Graham Goodchild

Model Aeroplanes of World War I

Design and Construction

B. T. Batsford Ltd, London

For Rachel

ISBN 0 7134 4896 2

Typeset by Katerprint Typesetting Services, Oxford
and printed in Great Britain by
The Bath Press
Bath, Somerset
for the publishers
B. T. Batsford Ltd
4 Fitzhardinge Street
London W1H 0AH

Contents

Acknowledgements

It would have been impossible to build the models for this book without reference to accurately drawn scale plans and technical information of the full size aircraft. I am therefore indebted to Model and Allied Publications Ltd for allowing me to base the drawings and models on their scale plans and also my wife Irene for typing the manuscript.

Introduction

Of all modelling pursuits, constructing model aircraft is probably the most popular and, indeed, can be traced back to the times of Leonardo Da Vinci, when models were used to test the theories of flight. The craft as we know it today, however, started in the early 1900s, although initially flying and display models were mainly built from plans and drawings. Simple wooden kits appeared in the mid 1930s and were produced until the early sixties when the plastics industry largely revolutionized the display model-kit market. For reasons of production economy, however, the choice of plastic kit is sometimes limited to the better known types of aircraft, and so often the modeller must build his or her own choice of model from plans using raw materials – a process otherwise known as 'scratch building'.

Scratch building model display aircraft of the First World War holds a particular fascination, both from a modelling viewpoint and an observational one. Their characteristic fabric-covered structures and rigging wires typify the antiquated charm of these historic old timers, and one has only to witness those fine museum models to testify to that. Armed with the techniques of building these models, you will have the freedom to construct any project at a modest cost and to a scale of your choice.

This book introduces the beginner to the various building techniques and tools required to construct from balsa wood, plastic card and wire, twelve First World War display models, including the famous Sopwith Camel, SE5a, and the Red Baron's Fokker Triplane. Photographs of the finished pieces are shown.

I General Principles of Construction

one
Tools and Adhesives

Gone are the days when one could whittle away at a piece of wood with just a penknife and some sandpaper. New materials and increasingly higher standards of model-making have necessitated a more comprehensive selection of tools. Although a well equipped workshop is not required, the introduction of specialized power tools over recent years has greatly improved efficiency and techniques.

The following hand tools listed here are fairly inexpensive to buy and are stocked by most hardware stores and model shops. Dividers and other drawing instruments can be obtained from art and graphic suppliers and some photocopying shops. The tools are categorized into three groups under the headings of, Model Aids, Construction, and Finishing and their uses explained.

Model Aids

Baseboard
One of the advantages of display models is that they are usually made to a fairly small scale, so that they can be built within a limited space, such as a table top or even a tea tray. Some sort of rigid baseboard, however, is very useful and can be constructed from either plywood or chipboard. A suitable size would be about 61cm (24in.) square and 12mm ($\frac{1}{2}$in.) thick. This should be large enough to construct models on and accommodate the tools and materials being used. When work is finished for the day, the board can be stowed away without the model being disturbed.

Building jig
This item is a useful aid for ensuring that the fuselage, tail-plane and wings are in correct alignment with one another, both in plan and front view. The jig consists of a baseboard of about twice the wingspan and the length of the fuselage of the model to be built. Glue a similar sized board at 90° to the rear edge of the base. Cover the base and back with graph paper, with the centre line ruled on in a contrasting colour such as red. Rule out longitudinal lines in blue ink on each side of the centre line at 1cm intervals towards the edges of the baseboard. Number these lines identically on each side of the centre line for easy reference when setting up the model. Finally, apply clear plastic self-adhesive film over the graph paper to protect the markings.

Building Jig

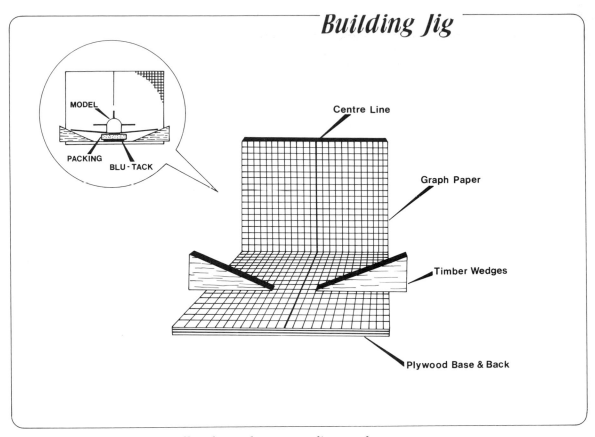

Place the fuselage centrally along the centre line and cut identical pairs of wooden wedges to support the wings and tail-plane. Move these in or out over the board until the correct angle (dihedral) is reached and glue the wings and tail-plane on. Also check that the fin is set up vertically by sighting it against the centre line on the back board.

Blu-Tack
Blu-Tack is very useful in modelling for temporarily holding small items—such as fuselage sides and frames—while you glue them together. It can also be used with cocktail sticks for holding parts while you paint, for forming cockpit padding during construction and fixing pilots in their seats.

Drawing board and tee and set squares
Drawing boards and tee and set squares are not required for the projects featured in this book, but they may be useful when you adapt your own plans for modelling. (For further details see Chapter 4 on scales and plans).

Magnifying glass
This is helpful when you are painting small items and putting in details, such as panel lines, stitching and cockpit interiors. A free-standing magnifying glass is best, mounted on a flexible arm to allow you to work with both hands.

Pins
These are used for general holding work and pinning down parts of fuselage constructed in balsa wood. They are also useful for supporting wings that are being painted before assembly.

Masking tape
This is also used generally for holding parts, while glue is setting, and masking off sections for painting.

Vice (pin and helping hands)
The *pin vice* grips drill bits in a pencil-like holder, and is rotated backwards and forwards between the thumb and forefinger to make small holes.

Helping hands
As the name implies this is a two armed articulated clamp, mounted on a free-standing cast iron stand. It is most useful for holding small items and models in fixed positions, leaving your hands free for applying details and rigging etc.

Construction tools

Drills
A normal set of high speed drill bits are adequate for all the materials used for these models. Use very small drill bits in the pin vice and a hand drill for the larger bits.

Files
These are mostly used for shaping and smoothing balsa wood fuselages and wings, and are also good for removing moulding flash on metal fittings and figures. A set should include rat-tail files for delicate work and flat, round and half-round files for larger work, as well as a rasp for rough, shaping work.

Glass paper
The finer grades are suitable for general smoothing of edges and surfaces of balsa wood and plastic card. Emery boards are excellent for very small parts and getting into corners when the end of the board is cut into a point.

Knives
I recommend two types: firstly, a general purpose knife for heavy cutting and carving—a Stanley knife, with standard replaceable blades and a firm handle, is ideal. Secondly, a knife for delicate cutting work is needed; this should have a fine pointed scalpel-type blade which is also replaceable, such as a Swann Morton Craft knife.

Plane
A small model makers' plane such as a razor blade-type is best for shaping and smoothing balsa wood fuselages; wings, tail-planes, and balsa wood wing cores on models made from plastic card.

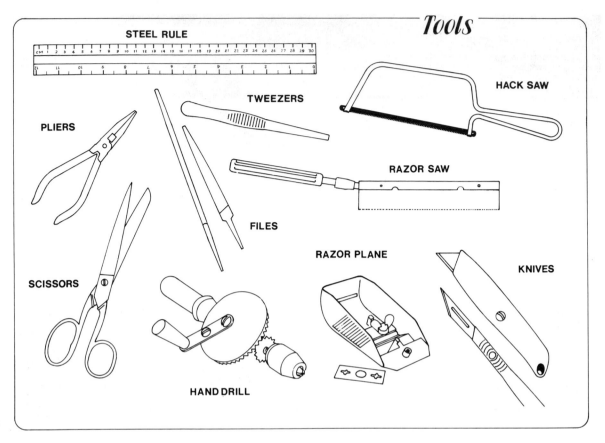

Tools

STEEL RULE

PLIERS

TWEEZERS

HACK SAW

RAZOR SAW

FILES

RAZOR PLANE

KNIVES

SCISSORS

HAND DRILL

Pliers
Pliers are mainly used for bending piano-wire to make wheel-axles and struts; a medium sized and a small, pointed nose pair should be adequate.

Saws
The modellers' razor saw is designed for cutting balsa wood and thick sheets of plastic card. Two or three different types of blade are available, which slot into an all-purpose handle. A small hacksaw will also be required for cutting piano-wire.

Scissors
A medium sized pair of good quality scissors are best for cutting paper, card, and thin sheets of plastic card. A small pointed pair are recommended for trimming the ends of rigging wires, plastic sprue, and thread.

Soldering iron
This is useful for joining piano-wire together or, when the model is to be motorized, for soldering electrical connections. You will need a soldering iron for two of the projects in this book for which I recommend a 25 watt iron.

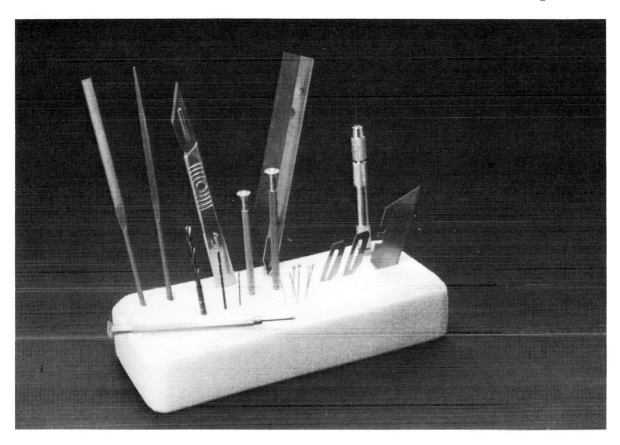

Straight edge
A steel rule of around 30cm (12in.) is suitable for cutting balsa wood and plastic card etc. with a knife.

Tweezers
These are essential for picking up and holding small items, I recommend a chisel edge and a pointed pair.

1 Foam block cut to hold tools and pins etc.

Finishing Tools

Brushes
Three sizes of brush are necessary for painting. The first two are chisel edge and are used for applying the base colours and cellulose dope on balsa wood models; preferable sizes are 6.0mm ($\frac{1}{4}$in.) and 9.0mm ($\frac{3}{8}$in.) You will need a brush for painting detail which has a fine point, preferably nylon, and is about 3.0mm ($\frac{1}{8}$in.) in size.

Cocktail sticks
Apart from their use in alcohol circles, these are useful in modelling circles for holding small items with dabs of Blu-Tack on one end while painting. The other pointed end of the sticks

are pushed into scrap pieces of wood for support while the paint dries. The sticks are also ideal for applying small amounts of glue.

Compasses
These are used for drawing on the roundel outlines on the wings and fuselage before painting. They are also used for drawing wheels and cowling faces onto balsa wood and plastic card during construction.

Dividers
Dividers are used to measure the lengths of rigging required before cutting it to length and gluing it in position and also for transferring the size of parts from the plan onto the material to be cut out.

Pencils and pens
A B or HB pencil is needed for marking on weathering and oil stain effects; stitching, panel lines, and other details such as cockpit instrument dials are inked on with a drafting pen such as a Rotring.

2 Drawing instruments for detailing and measuring.

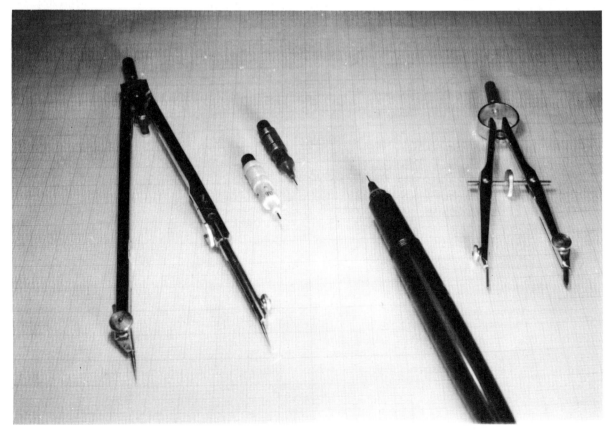

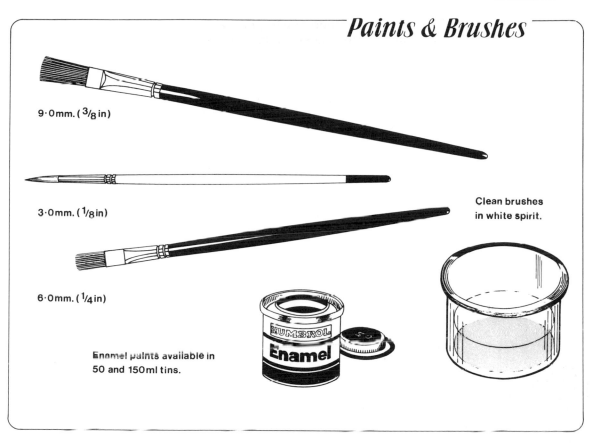

Paints & Brushes

9·0mm. (³/₈ in)

3·0mm. (¹/₈ in)

6·0mm. (¹/₄ in)

Clean brushes
in white spirit.

Enamel paints available in
50 and 150ml tins.

HUMBROL
Enamel

Adhesives

Balsa cement
This is most useful for joining balsa wood and can be used on ordinary card. It is fairly quick-setting but must be used sparingly on small models as it tends to shrink.

Contact adhesive
This is a powerful latex based glue applied to both surfaces to be joined. It is unsuitable for plastic card models as the glue erodes plastic. It is, however, useful in very small amounts when a quick bond is required such as when securing cockpit fittings in positions that are difficult to get at.

Epoxy adhesive
This is used to secure piano-wire struts and axles on balsa wood models. The wire or metal, however, must be thoroughly cleaned and scored with a file in order to achieve a good bond. When set hard, the adhesive can usefully be filed to any shape such as tail-skid support brackets. There are two sorts of adhesive packs available: normal hardening at 24 hours and rapid hardening at around 15 minutes (or even quicker with the application of heat).

Polystyrene adhesive

Available in tube and liquid solvent form, this is used to bond plastic card and styrene plastics in general. The tube form is used to seal the balsa wood wing cores on plastic card models before the plastic card wing-shells are fastened down onto double-sided adhesive tape. When thinned down with solvent the adhesive can be brushed over cockpit paddings moulded from Blu-Tack to form a hard shell for painting over.

The liquid solvent dissolves the surface of the plastic to be joined and is applied with its own brush applicator in the lid. It takes between 12 and 24 hours to set hard but parts can usually be handled carefully after a few minutes.

Polyvinyl acetate adhesive (P.V.A.)

This is a general purpose glue for most woods and will also hold together parts of dissimilar materials, which makes it very suitable for securing rigging wire, plastic, and thread. It is usually dispensed from a plastic bottle as a white liquid but it dries clear. For small items or for attaching rigging the glue is best applied with a cocktail stick. It takes about an hour to dry and 24 hours to set really hard, so enabling parts to be positioned without hurry.

Plastic filler

This is used on wood and plastic, but will erode plastic card if used in large amounts. It is better to build up small layers for filling any large holes. Polystyrene solvent can be used for thinning if necessary. The filler can also be used for moulding cockpit paddings and tyres for wheels.

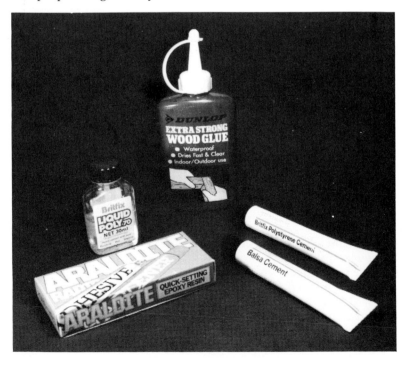

3 Selection of adhesives.

two

Materials and Techniques

Materials for constructing display models are various, unlike those for flying models where weight is a restricting factor. The exception to this is when display models are built on a production line basis, where for speed and economy plastic or metal parts only are produced from a master mould. For the model maker, however, constructing one-off display models at home with modest facilities, the more traditional materials, such as wood, card, and plastic card, can yield perfectly good results. The modeller's sole requirements are time and patience.

Most aircraft of the First World War period consist of fuselages of slab-sided, box-section type that are fairly straight forward to construct, using either wood, card, or plastic card, and are built up over transverse frames. Fuselages with curved sections are carved from solid wood. Wings can also be made from wood or plastic and are often built using both materials to

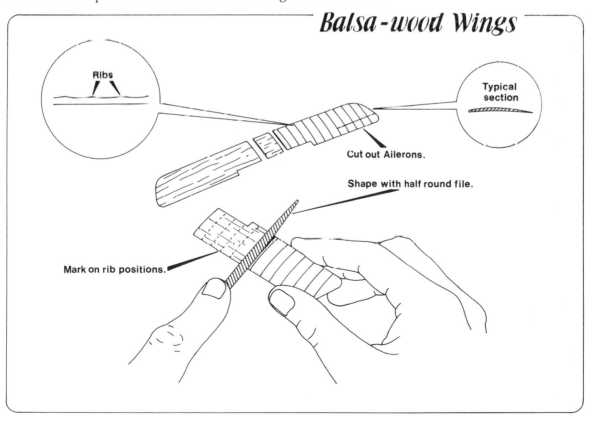

Balsa-wood Wings

Ribs

Typical section

Cut out Ailerons.

Shape with half round file.

Mark on rib positions.

form a sandwich construction. Propellers are normally carved from wood to emulate the full sized ones on aircraft, or ready made metal castings can be obtained commercially, together with rotary-type engines.

Listed below are the materials used to build the models in this book, including an explanation of the techniques used. Most of these materials are obtainable through local model suppliers; however, for specialized items some addresses are given in the appendix.

Balsa wood

This is the most widely used modelling material owing to its combined strength and lightness and also the ease with which it can be cut and shaped. It is available in sheet and block form in standard lengths of 91cm (36in.). Standard sheet width is 7.6cm (3in.) and it varies in thicknesses from 0.8mm ($\frac{1}{32}$in.) to about 6.0mm ($\frac{1}{4}$in.). Balsa block is available in various sizes including 25 × 25mm (1 × 1in.) square, which is used on some models in this book.

No special techniques are called for in using balsa wood other than taking care when cutting the thinner sheets so as not to split the grain. This can be avoided by cutting in from each end of the part to be cut out and also pointing the cutting knife in slightly towards the straight edge when cutting with the grain to prevent the knife diverging. Choose the softer grade of block for carving fuselages and harder grade of sheet for the propeller, wings and tail-plane.

Plastic card (Plasticard)

This material has largely taken over completely from ordinary card and is just as easy to fabricate. Its main advantage is that it can be moulded with heat, and very little preparation is required before painting. Sheets are available in A4 size and range in thicknesses from 0.25mm (0.010in.) to 2.00mm (0.80in.).

Slab sided fuselages

These are built up with the thicker sheets as you would do with balsa wood sheets. The parts to be cut out are lightly scored two or three times with a knife so they will snap out. Thinner sheets are suitable for curved sections and can be bent either by scoring or heating against a light bulb. Fuselage sections are held together with Blu-Tack and tape; solvent is then applied to the inside joints and left to set.

Wings

These are constructed around a balsa wood core with the rib detail scored from inside of the plastic card sheet; folded along the leading edge with the aid of heat from a fan heater and

Composite Plastic card / Wood Construction

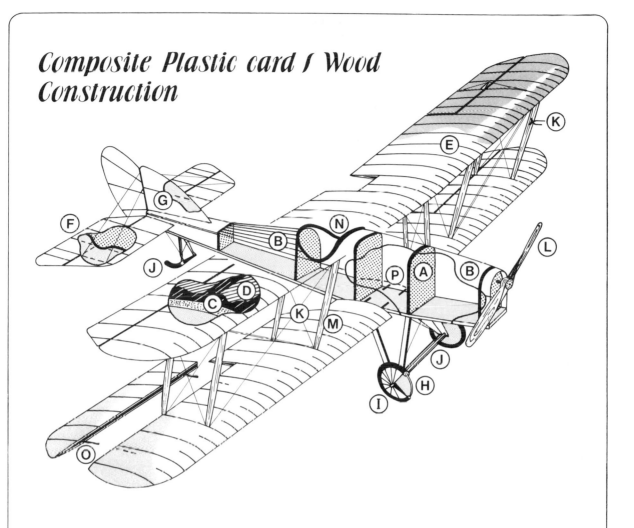

(A)	Fuselage frames	(I)	Moulded wheel covers
(B)	Thin plastic card covering	(J)	Plastic rod or sprue
(C)	Balsa~wood wing cores	(K)	Rolled wire or spruc
(D)	Double sided adhesive tape	(L)	Carved wood propeller
(E)	Rib detail scored from inside	(M)	Wood or plastic struts
(F)	Laminated tailplane (3 layers)	(N)	Rolled plastic filler padding
(G)	Laminated fin & rudder (2 layers)	(O)	Wire hinges
(H)	Laminated wheels & tyres (3 layers)	(P)	Wire wing lugs

Techniques

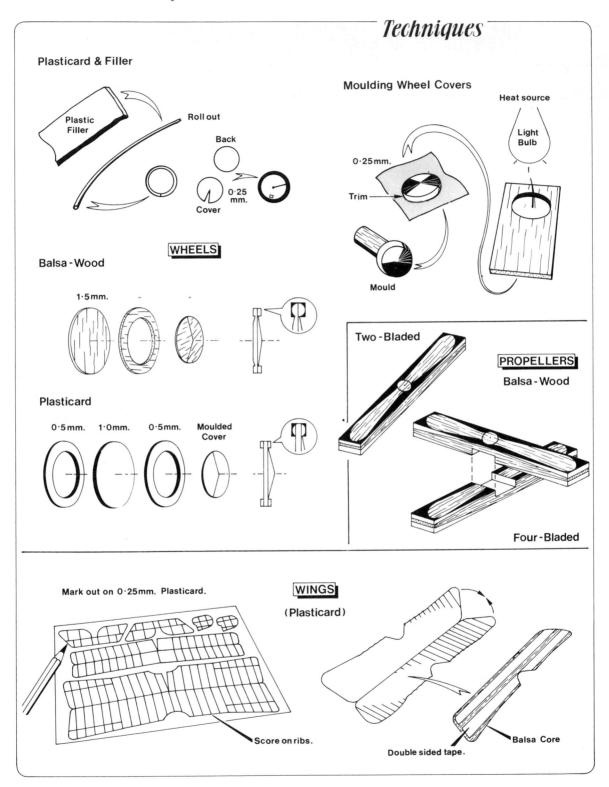

Plasticard & Filler

Plastic Filler

Roll out

Back

0·25 mm.

Cover

Moulding Wheel Covers

Heat source

Light Bulb

0·25mm.

Trim

Mould

WHEELS

Balsa-Wood

1·5mm.

Plasticard

0·5mm.   1·0mm.   0·5mm.   Moulded Cover

PROPELLERS

Two-Bladed

Balsa-Wood

Four-Bladed

Mark out on 0·25mm. Plasticard.

WINGS

(Plasticard)

Score on ribs.

Double sided tape.

Balsa Core

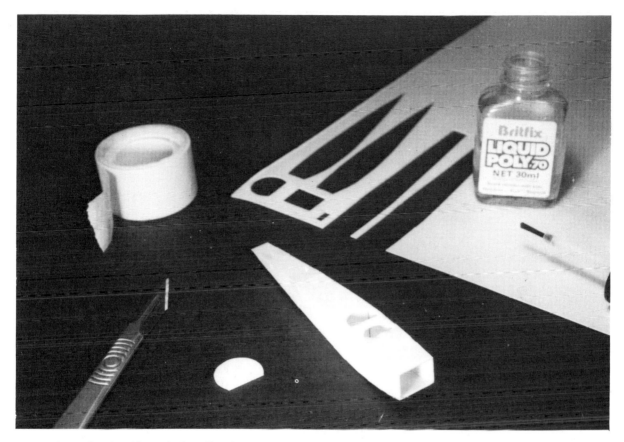

secured with double-sided adhesive tape. Solvent is then applied to the edges and left to set.

4 Fuselage being constructed from plastic card.

Wheel covers

Wheel covers and other small repetitive items can be moulded by making a male plug of the part and pushing into a female plug, cut out a little larger than the male plug, with thin plastic card in between, against a light bulb to soften the plastic.

Plastic rod and sprue

This is available in 30cm (12in.) lengths in packs of assorted sizes ranging from fine to about 1.50mm (0.060in.) in diameter. It is used for making wing and undercarriage struts on plastic card models. The finer lengths are used for rigging by measuring the distance between the wing struts with a pair of dividers and cutting the rod (or sprue as the finer lengths are called) to the measured length and gluing to the struts with P.V.A. glue. Other uses for plastic rod are: wheel-axles, propeller shafts, tail-skids, gun barrels, and various cockpit details.

Sprue can also be made at home by gently pulling and twisting a length of rod over a candle flame. It takes a little practice to

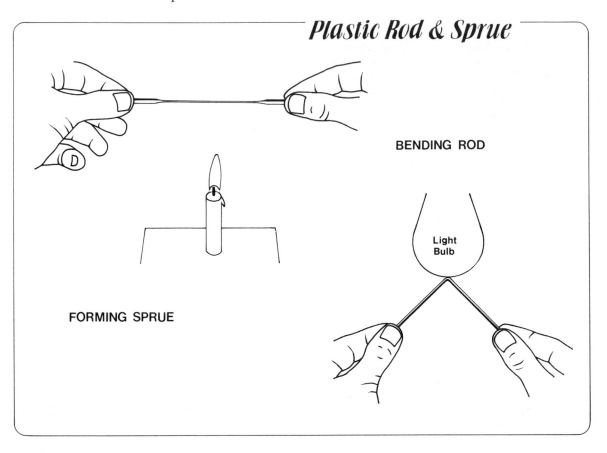

Plastic Rod & Sprue

BENDING ROD

Light Bulb

FORMING SPRUE

achieve good results, but very fine filaments can be obtained in this way.

Piano-wire

This is produced in standard 91cm (36in.) lengths and comes in various gauges (termed g or swg) from about 22g, 0.8mm ($\frac{1}{32}$in.) upwards. This is used for making wing lugs, struts and wheel-axles on balsa wood models.

Fuse-wire

Household fuse-wire, obtainable in packs of 5 to 30 amp. wire, is very suitable for making various fittings such as control columns and levers, gun mountings, push rods and exhausts on engines, and footsteps etc. The 5 amp. wire is suitable for making rigging by rolling the wire flat with a steel rule on a smooth surface and cutting to length using the same method as measuring plastic sprue.

Tubing

Any type of alloy, brass, or plastic small-bore tube is suitable for engine breather pipes and gun pivot mountings. Where rotary engines are required to rotate, tubing is slipped over the propeller shaft and glued through a pre-drilled hole in the cowling face or through the rear bulkhead.

Dowel

The smaller diameter balsa and birch dowel is suitable for making water-jacketed cylinders on in-line engines, and the larger diameters for crankcases on rotary engines. Plastic runners from kits can also be used to make cylinders when cut to length.

Steel bolts

These are perhaps an unlikely source of material but when they are cut down and the heads removed they make excellent cylinders, complete with cooling fins for rotary-type engines. The bolts are glued into pre-cut slots in the end of the balsa or birch dowel that forms the crankcase. Normally nine bolts make an engine. The dowel is then cut through just behind the bolts resulting in a basic engine to which the pushrods and other details are added.

5 Rotary type engine constructed from cut down bolts.

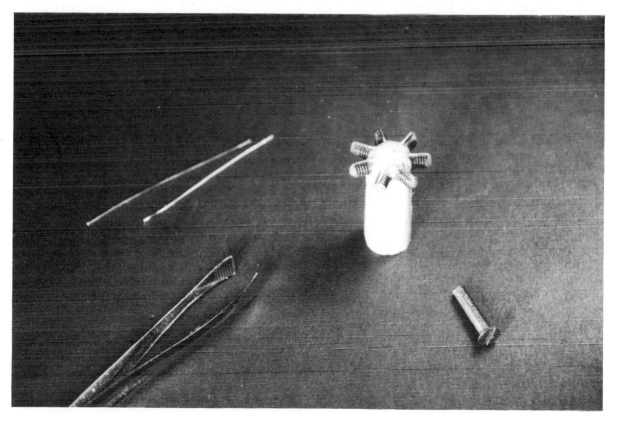

Thread

This is one method of making rib details on balsa wood wings and also battens and footruns on fuselages. Polyester yarn or nylon fishing line is superior to ordinary thread as there is no fluff deposit.

Paper

You can also use this for making rib details by cutting a sheet into narrow strips and gluing it with P.V.A. glue on the wings. Thicker paper or thin card is suitable for making pilot seats.

Light weight tissue, of the type used on flying model aircraft, is sometimes used for marking on camouflage details before the surface of balsa wood models is coated with dope. It is also suitable as a covering to seal the grain before painting.

Clear acetate sheet

This is used for making windscreens; it can be cut with scissors or a knife and fixed with P.V.A. glue.

6 Applying polyester yarn ribs to balsa wood wings.

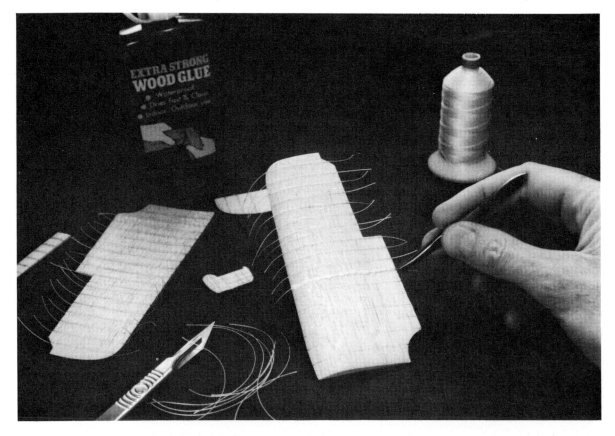

three
Finishing and Detailing

Preparation

In general, when building these type of aircraft, it is better to paint and detail the fuselage and wings separately before assembly, otherwise you may have difficulty in painting between the wings, especially around the centre section.

For models made from balsa wood, or any other timber, surfaces must be made as smooth as possible; carefully sand them with fine glass paper and repair all holes and blemishes. Cellulose sanding sealer is applied with a flat, moderate size brush to seal the grain and provide a firm, blemish-free surface on which to paint. Two or three coats may be necessary and must be smoothed down between each coat until a satisfactory finish is achieved. Small items such as struts and propellers will probably only require a single coat of sealer. In the case of propellers that require staining with wood dye, this must be applied first before sealing and finally finished with one or two coats of clear varnish.

In comparison very little preparation is necessary on plastic card models. All corners should be smoothed and rounded where required, using either fine glass paper or emery board. The trailing edges of the wings and tail-plane should be almost paper-thin, and this applies to wooden models as well. Any grease marks due to handling will affect painting; remove these with detergent.

Painting

Paints are available from most model suppliers. The Humbrol range of enamel paints for models are probably the most popular. These are obtainable in small tins of gloss, metallic, satin and matt finish. Clean your brushes in a small jam jar quarter-filled with white spirit; this should not require changing again until the model is almost completed as the paint from the brush separates after a few minutes and forms a sediment at the bottom of the jar, thus leaving the spirit clear to clean more brushes. Paints must be thoroughly stirred to dissolve all traces of sediment and lumps, and the lid replaced after use. Further stirring may be necessary during use.

Obviously each type of aircraft has its own particular colour scheme, although the same painting procedure applies more or less to all aircraft. Firstly, the insides of engine and gun wells, and cockpits are painted; usually you would use matt black for

engine wells and green for gun wells and cockpits. It is not critical if paint overlaps onto the fuselage as this can be painted over when the overall colours are applied. The lightest colour is applied first, usually to the underside of the aircraft, or all over if necessary. Use a flat brush, the largest that is practical. Two coats may be necessary to obtain an even covering. Darker colours and camouflage markings are then applied with the same size brush, or a small pointed brush to get into corners and obtain an even edge. Paint wheels and engines before fitting. (Cocktail sticks are ideal for holding wheels while the tyres are being painted.)

7 Cocktail sticks and 'helping hands' type clamp used to hold model and small items while painting.

Detailing

Cockpit details should at least consist of a pilot's seat, control column, throttle lever, priming pump, and rudder bar if it can be seen when no pilot figure is fitted. All these items, including machine guns, can be made from scrap plastic card, sprue, and fuse-wire, which are painted and glued in position. Instrument dials are picked out with either a pencil or a ruling pen, as are panel lines on the fuselage. A small, straight edge cut from plastic card is a suitable aid for this and also a cocktail stick, cut down and held on the end of a knife for awkward areas. Rivets on inspection hatches are shown by pressing a blunt pin on the

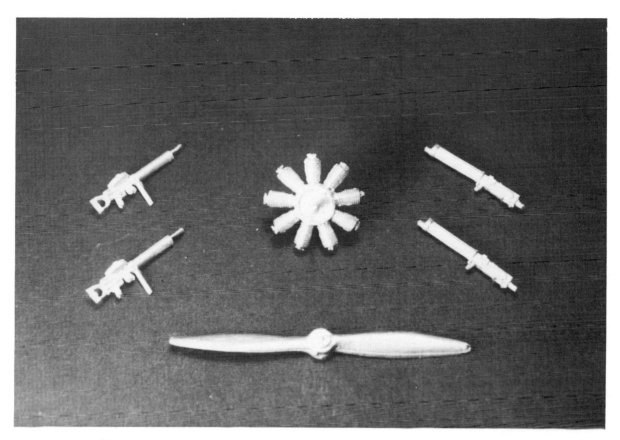

inside of thin Plasticard, painted and glued in place. This same
method can also be used for showing retaining nuts on propeller
bosses, or, instead, cut and glue on minute lengths of sprue for
retaining nuts.

8 Selection of bought white
metal fittings.

Transfers

Applying the transfers is the next step after gluing the remaining wings in position. On certain aircraft, however, it may be
easier to apply the transfers first. There are cases where roundels or crosses are not quite the correct size and the modeller
must mark and paint his or her own. A pair of compasses is
used to mark on roundels and then carefully painted with a
small pointed brush, using white as the base colour, followed by
the remaining colours when dry. Mark crosses on with black ink
and a ruling pen, by using a small straight edge, or, alternatively, cut a stencil from thin plastic card.

The Microscale make of transfers offers a range to suit most
aircraft types in the $\frac{1}{72}$nd and $\frac{1}{48}$th scales. These are of the water
slide type, which means that they have to be immersed in water
to release the image from the gummed-paper backing. Cut the
subject required from the sheet and dip it into a saucer of water
until the image slides from its backing; then apply it to the
model with tweezers. Swab off excess water with a tissue,
removing any trapped air bubbles and leave to dry. Where

transfers bridge control-surfaces on the wings and rudder, slit the transfer along the hinge line with a sharp knife or razor blade and smooth the edges into the recess. Dry letter transfers are also suitable for registration letters and numerals and can either be applied directly to the model, or pressed onto the non-sticky side of clear adhesive tape, cut out and stuck on. This method is useful when making up several digit numbers. Finally the entire model is given a coat of matt or semi-matt clear varnish depending on the finish required. This not only protects the transfers and panel lines but also gives the model a more authentic look.

Weathering
Weathering effects can further enhance the appearance of some models and are almost an artform in themselves. General dirt and oil stains are shaded on using a soft pencil and smudged with your finger or an eraser until the right effect is achieved, and then clear varnished. Sections to be considered for treatment are: around the engine cowling apertures, exhausts and breather pipes, footsteps, cockpit padding, and leading edges of wings. Rubber tyres are not supposedly black, but light grey when new. With use, however, they become dirty with the side walls retaining almost the original colour. Again this effect is obtained with smudged pencil. Mud splashes on wheels and

fuselages are achieved with minute dabs of brown paint applied with a dry brush. Whilst on the subject of wheels, the positions of these do differ according to whether the model is to be displayed in the sitting or flying position. In the flying position they are straight, but in the sitting position the wheels on some full sized aircraft splay out owing to the rubber suspension taking the weight of the aircraft.

Rigging

The same method of application applies to both sprue and wire rigging; on biplanes first measure and cut the diagonal lengths at the centre section struts across the wing chord and glue them, working out towards each wing tip. Next apply the diagonal span-wise rigging between the struts, again starting at the centre section and working on the front and rear sides of the wings towards the tips.

Pin holes are made in the fuselage and wings into which the control wires, and the sprue or wire is inserted with the remaining ends cut and glued to the control horns. The drag wires, glued between the wings and fuselage, are the last piece of rigging to be applied. Monoplanes in comparison have little or no rigging wires, with the exception of wing warping control-wires on some aircraft—and also undercarriage bracing, which is applied first of all.

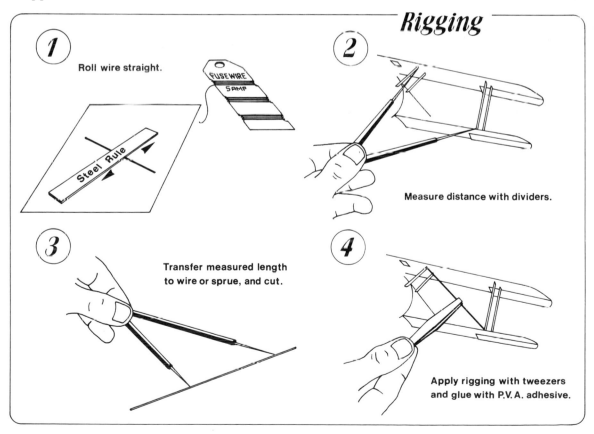

Rigging

1 Roll wire straight.

FUSEWIRE SAMP

Steel Rule

2 Measure distance with dividers.

3 Transfer measured length to wire or sprue, and cut.

4 Apply rigging with tweezers and glue with P.V.A. adhesive.

four

Scales and Plans

Scales

Scale is a measure of the reproduced reduction of the full sized aircraft. This can be shown in the form of a drawing or a model constructed to a specific size. The $\frac{1}{72}$nd scale—equal to one inch to six feet on the original—is the most popular scale that plastic kits are manufactured in, and is also suitable for scratch building. Models in this scale take up very little room when completed and details show up well. The $\frac{1}{48}$th scale—equal to $\frac{1}{4}$ inch to one foot is also popular—however, fewer plastic kits are available in this scale. Detailing offers extra scope for the scratch builder, and this larger scale does make handling the smaller parts easier. Other sizes include the $\frac{1}{24}$th and $\frac{1}{32}$nd scales, where really fine detailing can be shown.

The plans in this book are all drawn to just under $\frac{1}{48}$th scale with the exception of the Felixstowe F2A, which is drawn to just

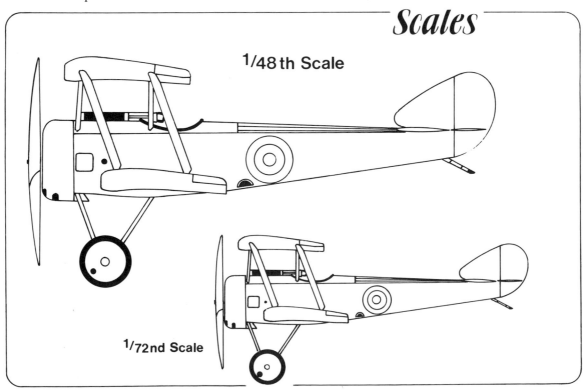

Scales

1/48th Scale

1/72nd Scale

under $\frac{1}{72}$nd scale. Enlargements or reductions in scale are best done photographically, either at home with a suitable camera using slide film, projecting the image onto paper and tracing it, or by having the plan photostated to the required size at a local photocopying shop.

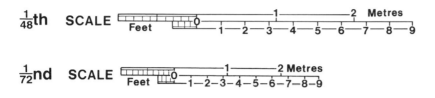

Plans

Aviation and model magazines often feature scale plans of full sized aircraft, including cross-sections and other details. It is up to the scratch builder, however, to interpret the plans according to which method of construction is chosen.

As mentioned earlier, the slab-sided fuselages are built up over frames that are drawn from selected cross-sections shown on the plan. Normally, frames are required where major changes in the shape of the fuselage occur. Generally frames are drawn for the two middle sections, a front, and a rear section; they are equally spaced in order to give adequate support. When marking out the frames from the sections, allowance has to be made for the thickness of the wood or Plasticard sides etc. A drawing board and tee and set squares are assets here; a straight edge and set square, however, are also suitable.

Fuselages
When these are carved from solid timber they do not require frames for support, and, therefore, the cross-sections on the plan are used only to check the shape using card templates as carving progresses.

The plans in this book are drawn showing all the necessary modelling construction details, including the actual size of frames etc. where appropriate, for tracing directly onto the material to be cut out (using carbon paper). The material and

MATERIAL AND SIZES KEY

BALSA SHEET		PLASTIC CARD		PLASTIC ROD		WIRE	
m.m.	in.	m.m.	in.	m.m.	in.	PIANO s.w.g.	FUSE amp.
①► 0·8	1/32	⑧► 0·25	0·010	⑭► 0·50	0·020	⑲► 22	㉓► 5
②► 1·5	1/16	⑨► 0·38	0·015	⑮► 1·00	0·040	⑳► 20	㉔► 15
③► 2·5	3/32	⑩► 0·50	0·020	⑯► Sprue		㉑► 18	㉕► 20
④► 3·0	1/8	⑪► 1·00	0·040	DOWEL		㉒► 44 Copper	㉖► 30
⑤► 6·0	1/4	⑫► 1·50	0·060	m.m.	in.	STEEL BOLTS	
⑥► 9·0	3/8	⑬► 2·00	0·080	⑰► 3·0	1/8	m.m.	in.
⑦► 25×25	1×1sq.			⑱► 9·0	3/8	㉗► 2·5	3/32

sizes used on the model are shown numerically and correspond with a common key at the bottom of each plan that lists the materials and sizes in metric and imperial equivalents. (Conversions are approximate, and sizes indicated are those that are generally available.)

Research

For the serious modeller who requires complete authenticity, magazines and books provide an invaluable source of information for research. Libraries and museums are another source for obtaining reference material, where a notebook and camera are useful for taking notes or making sketches, and photographing details such as cockpit interiors, armaments, and undercarriage arrangements etc. Always check first, however, that photography is allowed and, if necessary, get permission. Also take a tape measure along with you for recording the size of smaller items that are to be modelled.

II Model Projects

five
Fokker DVIII

Introduction

With its cantilever parasol wing the aircraft, known as the flying razor blade, represented quite a contrast compared with many of its biplane counterparts of the time. The fabric-covered fuselage consisted of a box-section, welded tube-structure, internally braced with piano-wire, and supporting a plywood covered wing. The DVIII entered service late in the war and after a series of fatal crashes due to wing failure, caused mainly by unseasoned timber components and shoddy workmanship, went on to become a potent fighter.

The single wing and simple lines of the fuselage makes the DVIII an ideal model to begin with. The fuselage, of sheet balsa wood, is made into a slab-sided box, supported by three frames. Balsa block is used for carving the engine cowling, and further sheet balsa is used for carving out the wing, tail-plane and propeller.

10 Fokker DV111.

Materials

Fuselage, 1.5mm ($\frac{1}{16}$in.), and 0.8mm ($\frac{1}{32}$in.) sheet balsa.
Wing, 6.0mm ($\frac{1}{4}$in.) sheet balsa.
Tail-plane and fin, 1.5mm ($\frac{1}{16}$in.) sheet balsa.
Propeller and axle fairing, 3.0mm ($\frac{1}{8}$in.) sheet balsa.
Cowling, 25mm (1in.) square balsa block.
Engine block, 9mm ($\frac{7}{8}$in.) balsa dowel.
Engine cylinders, cut from 2.5mm ($\frac{3}{32}$in) bolts.
Wing, tail-plane, undercarriage struts, and axle: 20 and 22
   gauge piano-wire.
Windscreen, clear acetate sheet.
Wheels, plastic card and filler.
Control wires, 5 amp. fuse-wire.
Control horns, 0.38mm (0.015in.) plastic card.

Construction

Trace and cut out from the plan the two fuselage sides and
frames, (A), (B), and (C), from 1.5mm ($\frac{1}{16}$in.) sheet balsa. Mark
the positions of the frames on the sides of the fuselage and glue
them together. Trace and cut out from 1.5mm ($\frac{1}{16}$in.) sheet balsa
the fuselage bottom and glue it to the bottom of sides and
frames. Trace and cut from 0.8mm ($\frac{1}{32}$in.) sheet balsa, formers
(A1), (A2), and (B1), (B2) and glue to both fuselage sides in line
with the frames.

11 Parts ready for sealing and
painting before assembly.

Trace and cut out from 0.8mm ($\frac{1}{32}$in.) sheet balsa the two fuselage side front sections and top, and glue over formers, holding with pins if necessary until set. Trim edges and fair the sides of the fuselage in flush where they finish at frame (C).

Carve the engine cowling from 25mm (1in.) square balsa block to the size and shape shown on the plan, and carve out the inside bottom section to take the engine. Drill out two 3mm ($\frac{1}{8}$in.) diameter holes in the front where shown and glue cowling to front of the fuselage. Trim and fair in flush with top and sides.

Trace and cut from 1.5mm ($\frac{1}{16}$in.) sheet balsa the tail-plane and fin, and glue centrally to the rear of the fuselage and fair in.

The rotary engine is constructed round a piece of 9mm ($\frac{3}{8}$in.) balsa dowel. Cut down 2.5mm ($\frac{3}{32}$in.) steel bolts to serve as the cylinders; these are epoxied into the dowel through pre-drilled holes with 22 gauge copper wire bent and epoxied to the cylinder sides to form the push rods. Only the bottom half of the engine will be seen through the cowling, so it is unnecessary to make all the cylinders.

Trace and cut out the wing from 6.0mm ($\frac{1}{4}$in.) sheet balsa; and the propeller from 3.0mm ($\frac{1}{8}$in.) sheet balsa. Taper the wing tips as shown and shape to an aerofoil section. Carve the propeller blades to the appropriate pitch, section for an anti-clockwise rotation and then smooth them down.

Shape the bucket seat bottom from 1.5mm ($\frac{1}{16}$in.) sheet balsa. Cut the back from thick paper and glue to the bottom edges.

Cut to length and bend the wing struts made from 20 gauge piano wire and epoxy them into the sides of the fuselage through pre-drilled holes. Trace and cut out from 3.0mm ($\frac{1}{8}$in.) sheet balsa the axle-fairing and shape to an aerofoil section. Cut a groove along the bottom and epoxy the 20 gauge piano-wire axle into it. Cut four lengths of 20 gauge piano-wire undercarriage struts as shown and epoxy into the bottom of the fuselage and top of the axle fairing through pre-drilled holes.

Finally, cut and bend the tail-skid from 22 gauge piano-wire and epoxy into the fuselage bottom through a pre-drilled hole. Apply epoxy glue near to the base and the tip of the skid. When set, file down the glue to form the skid support and the metal tip capping. The two remaining 20 gauge wing struts, wing, engine, propeller, and seat are fitted after the painting is finished. The wheels can be obtained commercially, or by constructing them on the method shown in the chapter on techniques.

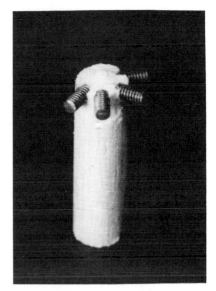

12 Construction of rotary engine.

Finishing

Smooth down all the external surfaces of the model with fine glasspaper, including, as far as possible, the inside of the cockpit and cowling. Apply two coats of sanding sealer and again smooth down. Try not to expose the grain with excessive rubbing. If it is exposed re-coat with more sanding sealer.

Transfers were used for the lozenge camouflage on the fuselage and the underside of the tail-plane. Cover the top first,

Fokker D.VIII.

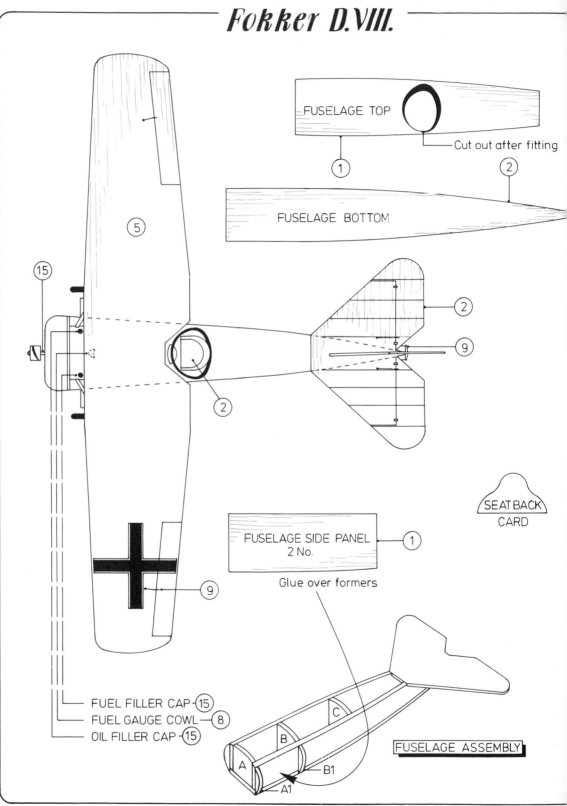

FUSELAGE TOP

Cut out after fitting

① ②

FUSELAGE BOTTOM

②

⑨

SEAT BACK
CARD

FUSELAGE SIDE PANEL
2 No.

①

Glue over formers

⑤

⑮

②

⑨

FUEL FILLER CAP ⑮
FUEL GAUGE COWL ⑧
OIL FILLER CAP ⑮

A
B
C
B1
A1

FUSELAGE ASSEMBLY

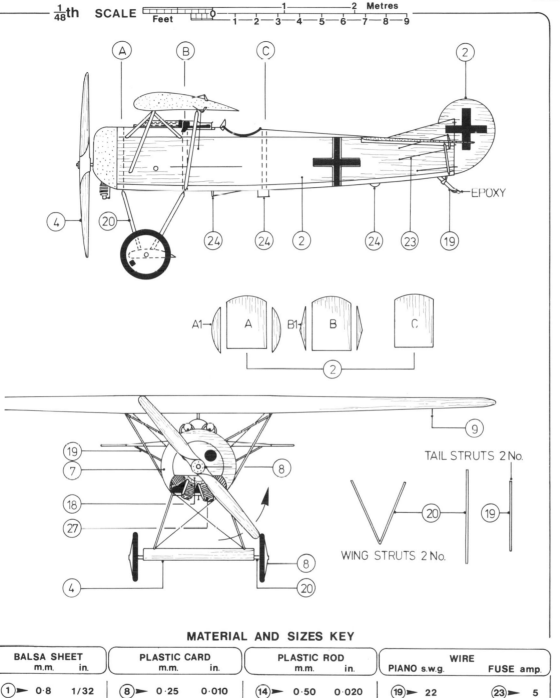

$\frac{1}{48}$th SCALE

Feet — Metres

EPOXY

A1 — A   B1 — B   C   2

TAIL STRUTS 2 No.

WING STRUTS 2 No.

MATERIAL AND SIZES KEY

BALSA SHEET m.m.	in.	PLASTIC CARD m.m.	in.	PLASTIC ROD m.m.	in.	WIRE PIANO s.w.g.	FUSE amp.
① 0·8	1/32	⑧ 0·25	0·010	⑭ 0·50	0·020	⑲ 22	㉓ 5
② 1·5	1/16	⑨ 0·38	0·015	⑮ 1·00	0·040	⑳ 20	㉔ 15
③ 2·5	3/32	⑩ 0·50	0·020	⑯ Sprue		㉑ 18	㉕ 20
④ 3·0	1/8	⑪ 1·00	0·040	DOWEL m.m.	in.	㉒ 44 Copper	㉖ 30
⑤ 6·0	1/4	⑫ 1·50	0·060	⑰ 3·0	1/8	STEEL BOLTS m.m.	in.
⑥ 9·0	3/8	⑬ 2·00	0·080	⑱ 9·0	3/8	㉗ 2·5	3/32
⑦ 25×25	1×1sq.						

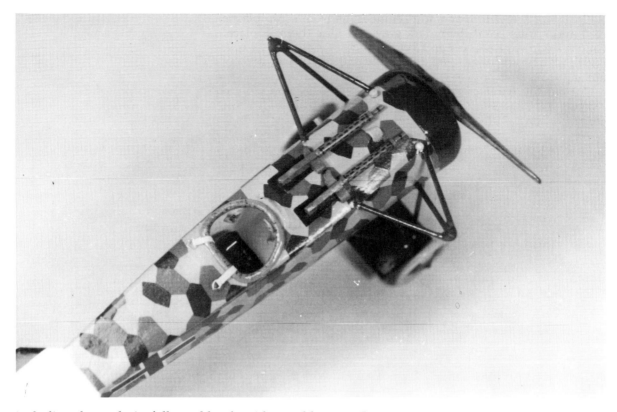

13 Top view before fitting wing.

including the cockpit, followed by the sides and bottom. It may be helpful if the sections are first traced onto paper before cutting out the transfers. Cut out the cockpit opening with a sharp knife and trim if necessary where the transfers meet the cowling. Also cover the wheel centres with lozenge transfers that are slit from the centre to facilitate covering.

Attach the cockpit padding, made from rolled Blu-Tack around the rim and seal with polystyrene cement diluted with solvent. Cut out the control horns from scrap, thin plastic card and glue to both sides of all the control surfaces.

Paint the wing, cowling, axle fairing, and struts with dark green enamel. The rudder, fin, and upper tail-plane surfaces are white, and tyres are painted light grey. Also painted grey are the handles, footstep (port side only), and the petrol and oil filler caps etc. These latter items are made from fuse-wire and scrap plastic rod, and glued where shown. Paint the engine crankcase and propeller boss silver. Clear gloss varnish is used on the cowling and propeller. Glue the engine in position and mount the propeller on a plastic rod shaft, glued into a pre-drilled hole in the cowling face and fasten the propeller with the plastic card boss. The cockpit padding and tail-skid are tan coloured with grey metal cap and support on the tail-skid.

Apply the cross insignia transfers where shown. The black strips on the tail-plane and the control surfaces were picked out with black ink using a ruling pen. Coat the entire model, except the cowling, with semi-matt clear varnish.

Construct the two Spandau machine guns from scrap plastic card and sprue; paint them dark grey and glue them in place. Glue the wing and wheels and the two remaining wing struts in position. Cut to length the control wires and undercarriage bracing from 5 amp. fuse-wire and glue in place.

Cut out the windscreen from clear acetate sheet and glue to the fuselage, together with the interior cockpit fittings, which consist of control column, rudder bar, throttle lever, and primer pump, all made from plastic sprue. The seat is painted green and seat belts are made from masking tape with fuse-wire buckles and glued into the cockpit.

six

Sopwith F1 Camel

Introduction

The Sopwith Camel is probably the best known aircraft of the First World War and was responsible for downing well over 1000 enemy aircraft. The name Camel evolved from the hump shaped fairing on top of the fuselage, housing the twin Vickers machine-guns. With its powerful rotary engine and fairly short fuselage the aircraft was tricky to handle, but unrivalled in its manoeuvrability in the hands of expert pilots. It was constructed with the usual wood-box girder fuselage, wire-braced internally, and spruce spar wings with tubular steel trailing edges and wing tips. Apart from the aluminium engine cowling and plywood cockpit decking, the entire airframe was covered with fabric. As with most aircraft of this period, the undercarriage axle was hinged in the middle and the wheels were suspended on elastic cord shock absorbers that took the weight of the aircraft under load, resulting in the wheels splaying out.

In order to cope with the hump and changing contours, the fuselage of the model is carved from solid balsa wood. The wings, cowling, tail-plane, and wheels are made from sheet balsa, and wing and undercarriage struts made from birch dowel.

14 Sopwith Camel.

Materials

Fuselage, 25 × 25mm (1 × 1in.) block balsa.
Wings, 3.0mm ($\frac{1}{8}$in.) sheet balsa.
Tail-plane, fin and wheels, 1.5mm ($\frac{1}{16}$in.) sheet balsa.
Engine cowling, 1.5mm ($\frac{1}{16}$in.) sheet balsa (laminated).
Propeller, 0.8mm ($\frac{1}{32}$in.) sheet balsa (laminated).
Wing and undercarriage struts, 3.0mm ($\frac{1}{8}$in.) birch dowel.
Undercarriage and tail-skid, 20 and 22 gauge piano-wire.
Controls and rigging wire, 5 amp. fuse-wire.

15 Fuselage and cowling carved to shape.

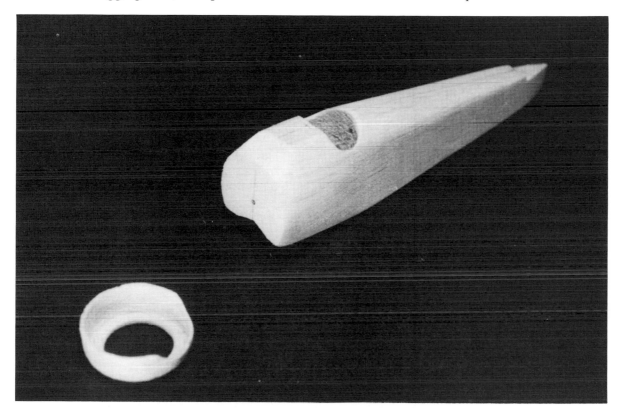

Construction

Cut a little longer than the length of the fuselage, a length of 25 × 25mm (1in. × 1in.) block balsa and trace the fuselage profile from the plan on to one side of the block. Using a razor-saw, plane and a file, cut and shape it to the outline, ensuring the edges are exactly at right angles with the profile. Mark the centre line on the top and bottom of the fuselage, together with stations (A) to (E), and mark on the widths of the fuselage from the sections shown on the plan. Cut out and shape as shown on the plan view, again keeping the sides square with the top and bottom. Shape the curved top decking and the hump to the outline shown on the sections. Note that the fuselage sides become progressively rounded from the flat sides at section (C) to a circular section at (A).

Sopwith F.1. Camel

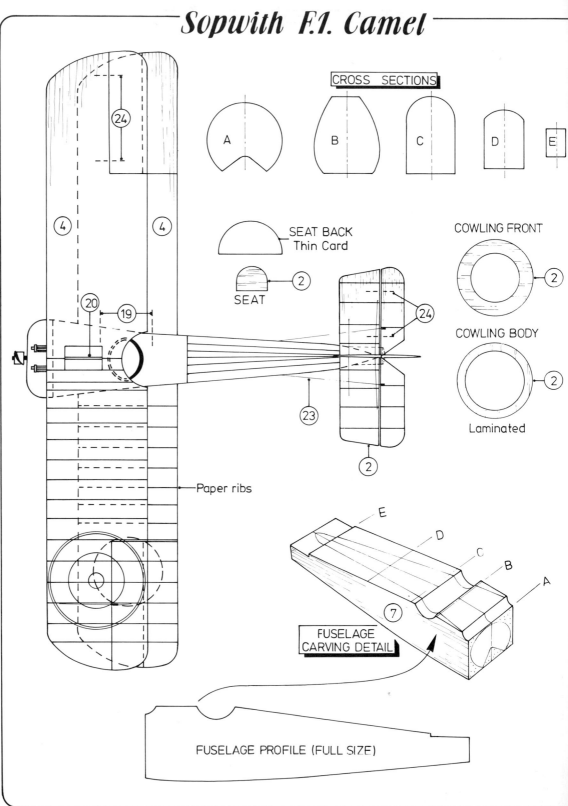

CROSS SECTIONS

A   B   C   D   E

SEAT BACK
Thin Card

SEAT

COWLING FRONT

COWLING BODY

Laminated

Paper ribs

FUSELAGE
CARVING DETAIL

FUSELAGE PROFILE (FULL SIZE)

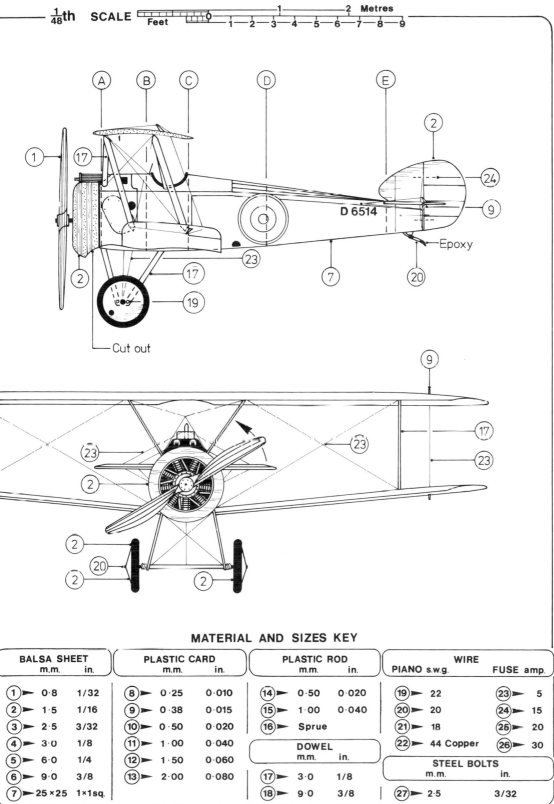

D 6514

Epoxy

Cut out

MATERIAL AND SIZES KEY

BALSA SHEET		PLASTIC CARD		PLASTIC ROD		WIRE			
m.m.	in.	m.m.	in.	m.m.	in.	PIANO s.w.g.		FUSE amp.	
① 0·8	1/32	⑧ 0·25	0·010	⑭ 0·50	0·020	⑲ 22		㉓ 5	
② 1·5	1/16	⑨ 0·38	0·015	⑮ 1·00	0·040	⑳ 20		㉔ 15	
③ 2·5	3/32	⑩ 0·50	0·020	⑯ Sprue		㉑ 18		㉕ 20	
④ 3·0	1/8	⑪ 1·00	0·040	**DOWEL**		㉒ 44 Copper		㉖ 30	
⑤ 6·0	1/4	⑫ 1·50	0·060	m.m.	in.	**STEEL BOLTS**			
⑥ 9·0	3/8	⑬ 2·00	0·080	⑰ 3·0	1/8	m.m.		in.	
⑦ 25×25	1×1sq.			⑱ 9·0	3/8	㉗ 2·5		3/32	

Carve out the vee at the base of section (A) and the inside of the machine-gun hump, cutting back from the front for a distance of about 9mm ($\frac{3}{8}$in.). Drill out the cockpit and carve to shape. The front top decking and sides should be about 1mm thick to allow room for the instrument panel. Smooth out the inside of the cockpit as far as possible and seal the grain with a layer of balsa cement. Cut out the step for the tail-plane to sit in and smooth down the outside of the fuselage with fine glasspaper.

Trace and cut out from 1.5mm ($\frac{1}{16}$in.) sheet balsa the five rings that make up the engine cowling. The front ring has a smaller inside diameter. Glue the rings together and when set carve out the inside to about 1mm in thickness. Round off the front of the cowling and smooth the exterior to match the body of the fuselage. Do not glue the cowling to the fuselage until the engine has been painted. Cut out the crescent-shaped air vent at the bottom and smooth down.

Trace and cut out from 3.0mm ($\frac{1}{8}$in.) sheet balsa the upper and lower wings and carve to an aerofoil section with under-camber and smooth down. Similarly trace and cut the tail-plane and fin from 1.5mm ($\frac{1}{16}$in.) sheet balsa and smooth down to an aerofoil section. Mark the positions of the ribs on all the flying surfaces. The ribbing effect is produced by cutting 1mm wide lengths of paper strip and gluing over the surfaces. Metric graph paper is suitable for this purpose as the lines are drawn 1mm apart. Mark on the positions of the ailerons and elevators and cut out and round off the leading edges. Similarly cut out and round off the leading edge of the rudder at the hinge line.

Mark the position of the lower wings on the sides of the fuselage and bevel the wing roots to the correct dihedral. Insert two lugs; cut these from 22g. piano-wire, push them into each wing root, press the protruding lugs into the sides of the fuselage, and glue. Hold the fuselage over the plan until the wings have set to maintain the correct dihedral. The wing and undercarriage struts are carved from 3.0mm ($\frac{1}{8}$in.) birch dowel. It is easier first to thin and shape a length of dowel and then cut the struts to the required lengths. Mark the positions of the four centre wing struts on top of the fuselage and glue into pre-cut slots at the correct angle. The front struts should be vertically in line with the front of the fuselage at section (A). Mark the positions of the remaining struts between the upper and lower wings and glue the struts only into the *lower* wings into pre-cut slots. The *upper* wing is glued on the struts after the painting is finished.

Glue the tail-plane into the step in the rear of the fuselage and fair in. Glue the fin centrally on top of the tail-plane after first shaping the base of the fin to sit over the curved surface of the tail-plane.

Mark the positions of the undercarriage struts on the fuselage and glue the struts into pre-cut slots, after first cutting them to correct lengths. Check from the plan that they are correctly splayed as you look at them from the front, and glue each pair of struts together where they meet at the axle position. Cut the axle

to length from 20g. piano-wire together with the two 22g. piano-wire axle supports, and glue them in place in between the struts.

The tail-skid is cut and bent as shown from 20g. piano-wire, and glued into a pre-drilled hole at the rear of the fuselage. Apply epoxy resin at the tip and file down when set to form the shape of the skid.

Cut the wheels from two laminations of 1.5mm ($\frac{1}{16}$in.) sheet balsa glued together. Each wheel consists of a disc and a further disc with the middle cut out to form the tyre. Smooth round to obtain the correct tyre profile and shape the cut out from the disc to make the hub and glue in place.

Very often the propellers on full sized aircraft were made from different timbers laminated together to give a striped appearance. This can be represented on the model by soaking strips of 0.8mm ($\frac{1}{32}$in.) sheet balsa in mahogany wood dye, laminated between natural sheet balsa, and then carved to shape. Alternatively, genuine mahogany veneer can be used. Sheet balsa (1.5mm ($\frac{1}{16}$in.)) is used for the bucket seat base, and thin card for the back. The rotary engine can be made from cut down 2.5mm ($\frac{3}{32}$in.) bolts epoxied into dowel or you could buy a white metal engine. It is better to install the engine after painting.

16 Parts ready for sealing and painting (note ribs made from strips of paper).

Finishing

Lightly smooth down the entire model with fine glasspaper, including the control surfaces, wheels, propeller and cowling. Feather down the edges of the paper ribs into the wing to form a curve, representing the natural sag of the fabric between the ribs on the full sized aircraft. Apply two coats of sanding sealer to all the balsa wood structure and smooth down. Repeat with a further coat. Stain the birch wing and undercarriage struts with mahogany dye and apply two coats of clear varnish to these and also the laminated propeller.

Fasten the control surfaces in the required positions with 15 amp. fuse-wire and glue. Cut out the ten control horns from 0.38mm (0.15in.) plastic card and glue them into pre-cut slots in the control surfaces. Roll out the cockpit padding from Blu-Tack and glue it around the rim of the cockpit, coating the padding with polystyrene cement diluted with solvent.

Cut out the footstep in the port side of the fuselage where shown and paint the inside matt black. Also paint the engine bulkhead and cylinders, and inside the gun cowling in matt black. Paint the cockpit interior light matt green and the underside of the fuselage and flying surfaces natural doped linen colour (beige). The upper flying surfaces, fuselage top and sides, including the fin, are painted in khaki green.

Apply the ribbing and other details on top of the fuselage with black ink and a ruling pen, aided with a straight edge. Lightly pencil in the rib positions on the underside of the flying surfaces. Apply the roundel transfers and other markings. The serial number is applied from a dry transfer lettering sheet.

Mark and paint silver the forward fuselage panels and cowling, including the engine crankcase. The exhaust pipes are burnt copper coloured. Paint the cockpit padding tan and the tail-skid natural wood colour with a grey metal tip. The tyres are also painted grey with the wheel centres and axle assembly in khaki green. Finally, apply a coat of clear matt varnish over all the painted surfaces, except the silver coloured cowling and forward fuselage panels, which are varnished with clear gloss.

Fasten the back of the engine through a pre-drilled hole in the front of the fuselage, followed by the cowling. If you want the engine to rotate, check that it is not binding on the cowling. File the cylinders down where they are not visible if necessary to free the engine. Glue the propeller on the shaft and the boss, made from thin plastic card, which is painted silver.

Cut out the windscreen from clear acetate sheet and glue in place; then glue on the two Vickers machine guns. If you intend using metal fittings for the guns, cut the barrels from the breaches and glue the barrels only into the hump and the rear ends of the breaches in the cockpit. The guns should be painted dark grey before they are fitted.

Glue the wheels to the axle in a splayed position if the model is to be shown at rest, or straight if in flying mode. The oval metal engine panels are cut out from baking foil and glued to the fuselage. Rivets in the panels are shown by lightly pressing a

ball-point pen on the reverse sides before they are glued in position.

Finally, glue on the upper wing and the rigging and control wires. Paint and glue in the pilot seat and add cockpit details as required. The instrument panel was drawn onto paper and stuck on plastic card. The seat belts are narrow strips of masking tape with fuse-wire buckles. Construct the pitot tube also from fuse-wire, glue it to the outer front starboard wing strut, and paint grey.

17 Ribs pencilled on underside of wings.

seven

Morane Saulnier Type L

Introduction

This parasol wing monoplane entered service at the beginning of the First World War, and typically conformed to the usual fabric-covered, wooden braced fuselage and wings, except for its aluminium cowling and plywood forward panels. Ailerons were not fitted; instead, the wing was made to flex via a series of control wires attached to the wing panels that ran over a pulley in the apex of the pylon, back under the fuselage to the vee structure, where, through cranks, the wires led up to the cockpit controls through the bottom of the fuselage.

Owing to the entire tail assembly being made to pivot, the aircraft was reportedly sensitive to handle. Early machines were powered by the seven cylinder 80 h.p. Gnome rotary engine, but were later superseded by the more reliable Le Rhône engine.

The only armament carried was hand held rifles for air to air combat. Bombs were lobbed out over the cockpit, or sometimes carried on improvized racks. Indeed, one of the first Victoria Crosses was earned when a pilot destroyed a Zeppelin by dropping bombs on it.

18 Morane Saulnier.

With its simple slab-sided fuselage, the aircraft makes a suitable modelling subject to begin plastic card building techniques. Plastic card is used for both the fuselage and flying surfaces, and plastic rod for the undercarriage and pylon. The engine is made from cut-down bolts, and the propeller and crankcase carved from balsa wood.

Materials

Fuselage and tail-plane, 0.50mm (0.020in.) plastic card.
Cowling, 0.38mm (0.015in.), and 1.00mm (0.040in.) plastic card.
Wing, 1.00mm (0.040in.) plastic card.
Undercarriage, pylon, and tail skid, 1.00mm (0.040in.), and 0.50mm (0.020in.) plastic rod.
Wheels, 0.25mm (0.010in.) plastic card and filler.
Engine cylinders, cut from 2.5mm ($\frac{3}{32}$in.) bolts, and 15 amp. fuse-wire.
Engine block, 9mm ($\frac{3}{8}$in.) balsa dowel.
Windscreen, clear acetate sheet.
Control wires, stretched plastic sprue.
Tail-plane hinge, 22 gauge piano-wire.
Propeller, 3.0mm ($\frac{1}{8}$in.) sheet balsa.

Construction

Trace and cut out from 0.50mm (0.020in.) plastic card: the sides of the fuselage—top and bottom, including frames, (A), (B), and (C)—the tail-plane, and fin.

Mark the positions of the frames on the inside of the fuselage sides and glue sides to the frames, checking that the sides are level with each other.

Tape the bottom and top to the sides of the fuselage and run solvent along the joints. Remove tape when this has set and smooth down corners with fine glasspaper.

Trace and cut out from 0.38mm (0.015in.) plastic card the combined cowling and deck. Locate and glue frame (A) onto the front of the fuselage and leave it to set. Tape the cowling around frame (A) and the deck to the sides of the fuselage and apply solvent to the joints. Cut the cowling front from the plan from 1.00mm (0.040in.) plastic card and glue it to the inside of the cowling. Hold with tape if necessary until it has set. Fair in the edges and smooth down. Trace and cut out the windscreen from clear acetate sheet and glue to the top of the fuselage, up against the curved edge of the deck.

Cut the wing from 1.00mm (0.040in.) plastic card, and file and smooth down to an aerofoil section. In order to give the wing the right amount of warp (curvature) score three lines along the top of the wing where shown on the plan, bend to shape, and apply solvent to the cuts. When set, smooth down.

On the full sized aircraft the whole of the tail-plane has a hinge joint. For the model, the pivot is made from 22g. piano-wire, cut to length and pushed through pre-drilled holes in the rear of the sides of the fuselage. Cut a slot in each tail-plane

Morane - Saulnier Type 'L'

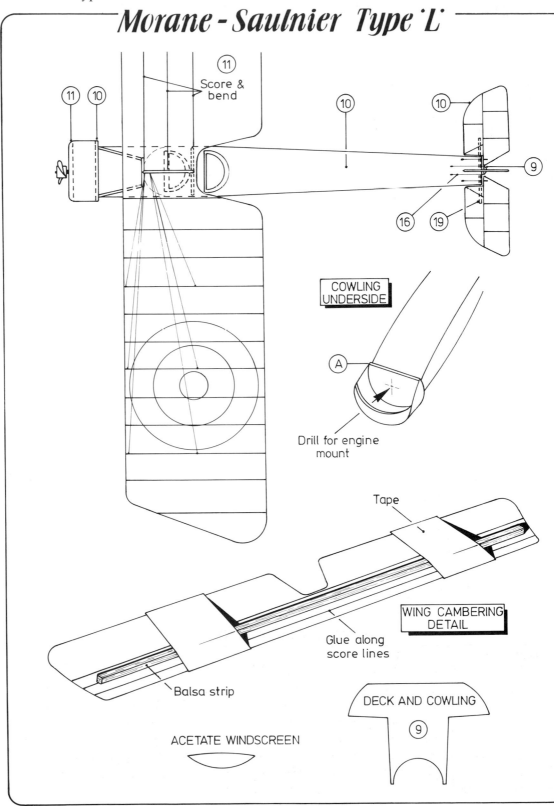

(11)
Score &
bend

(11) (10)

(10)

(10)

9

16   19

COWLING
UNDERSIDE

A

Drill for engine
mount

Tape

WING CAMBERING
DETAIL

Glue along
score lines

Balsa strip

ACETATE WINDSCREEN

DECK AND COWLING
9

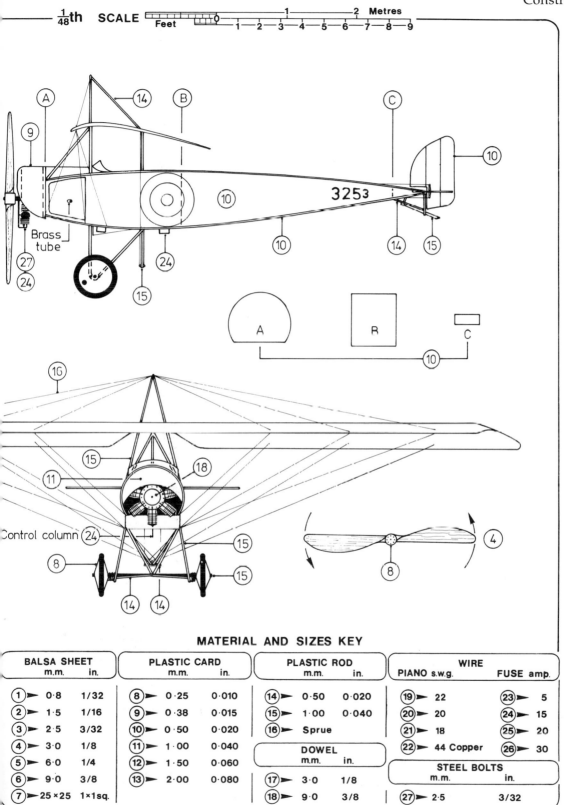

$\frac{1}{48}$th SCALE   Metres / Feet

Brass tube

Control column

3253

MATERIAL AND SIZES KEY

BALSA SHEET			PLASTIC CARD			PLASTIC ROD			WIRE			
	m.m.	in.		m.m.	in.		m.m.	in.	PIANO s.w.g.		FUSE amp.	
①	0·8	1/32	⑧	0·25	0·010	⑭	0·50	0·020	⑲	22	㉓	5
②	1·5	1/16	⑨	0·38	0·015	⑮	1·00	0·040	⑳	20	㉔	15
③	2·5	3/32	⑩	0·50	0·020	⑯	Sprue		㉑	18	㉕	20
④	3·0	1/8	⑪	1·00	0·040		DOWEL		㉒	44 Copper	㉖	30
⑤	6·0	1/4	⑫	1·50	0·060		m.m.	in.	STEEL BOLTS			
⑥	9·0	3/8	⑬	2·00	0·080	⑰	3·0	1/8		m.m.		in.
⑦	25×25	1×1sq.				⑱	9·0	3/8	㉗	2·5		3/32

where shown and glue them to the protruding piano-wire in the required position (either down for stationary or horizontal for flying). The control horns are cut from 0.38mm (0.015in.) plastic card and glued to the upper and lower surfaces of the tail-plane at the hinge, and to each side of the rudder.

Mark the position of the four undercarriage struts on the fuselage, and cut the four struts to length from 1.00mm (0.040in.) plastic rod and shape to an oval section. Glue each pair of struts to form a vee into pre-drilled holes on each side of the fuselage where marked. Cut to length the axle from 1.00mm (0.040in.) plastic rod, and glue between the two inside apex's of the vees. Glue between the struts the axle supports, cut from 0.50mm (0.020in.) plastic rod, and glue the central undercarriage vee strut, cut from 1.00mm (0.040in.) plastic rod, between the front axle support and the fuselage where the forward struts enter the fuselage. Cut the tail skid and support from plastic rod as specified and glue in position, together with the rudder. The skid itself should be shaped first before gluing.

Mark on top of the fuselage the positions of the six centre section wing struts and drill holes appropriately. Cut to length the struts from 1.00mm (0.040in.) plastic rod, rounded to an oval section and glue into position to form an inverted vee on each side of the fuselage. They should lean inwards as shown, with the rear struts vertically in line with the front legs of the under-

19 Cockpit and centre section detail.

carriage. Glue the rear centre struts in place, together with a piece of 1.00mm (0.040in.) plastic card for support under the fuselage deck between the two cockpit openings.

Position the wing on top of the struts and mark; glue the wing to the struts through pre-drilled holes. Cut appropriate lengths of 0.50mm (0.020in.) plastic rod for the pylon and glue them on top of the lower struts protruding through the wing.

The lower control wire vee strut is made from 1.00mm (0.040in.) plastic rod and glued between the rear undercarriage legs. Plastic rod measuring 0.50mm (0.020in.) is used to make the cranks, which are then glued to each side of the apex of the vee.

Construct the rotary engine round a piece of cut down 9mm ($\frac{3}{8}$in.) balsa dowel for the crankcase and cut down 2.5mm ($\frac{3}{32}$in.) steel bolts for the cylinders. Form the push rods out of 15 amp. fuse-wire and epoxy them in place. Trace and cut out the propeller from 3.0mm ($\frac{1}{8}$in.) sheet balsa, and carve and smooth to shape. The bucket seats can be made from sheet balsa or plastic card and fitted after painting. Unless absolute authenticity is required, only the rear seat need be made, as this can easily be seen through the centre section wing cut out.

The wheels on the model were constructed from 0.25mm (0.010in.) plastic card for the hubs and the tyres formed out of plastic filler.

Finishing

The model represented here is of Warneford's aircraft with which he won the Victoria Cross in for destroying a Zeppelin. The over all finish is natural linen colour (beige) with the exception of the forward timber panels, which are light brown, and aluminium coloured cowling. All struts and pylons are black. The wheels are natural linen coloured with grey tyres. The engine crankcase and propeller boss are silver and are made from thin plastic card.

Cut and bend the foot steps from 15 amp. fuse-wire and glue into pre-drilled holes in the underside of the fuselage. Brass tubing is used for the breather pipe and glued into a pre-drilled hole in the port engine panel. These later items are painted grey, together with the lower pylon cranks and metal-tipped, tan coloured tail-skid.

Transfers can be used for the French insignia roundels, although in this case these were painted on by hand, as were the vertical blue, white, and red tail stripes. Different sized figures on dry transfer sheets were used for the serial number, and panel lines were inked on with a ruling pen. The rib detail on the wings and tail-plane is marked on with a pencil, aided by a straight edge, and the surfaces, including the fuselage, coated with semi-gloss clear varnish. Apply gloss varnish to the cowling and propeller, which is stained with mahogany dye, and matt varnish on the wheels.

Fasten the engine inside the cowling. This can be fixed permanently with glue or made to rotate by slipping a piece of brass tubing over the shaft and gluing through a pre-drilled hole in the bulkhead. Glue the propeller to the shaft together with the boss, and finally the wheels on the axle. The wheels should splay out slightly if the model is to be shown at rest.

Plastic sprue is used for all the control and rigging wires, and is measured beforehand with a pair of dividers and glued in place, starting with bottom wires, followed by the top, and finally the crank and tail-plane control wires.

If the wing is not flat, tape on a balsa wood splint until the sprue has been applied and then remove the splint.

eight
Hansa Brandenberg W-29

Introduction

The W-29 monoplane entered service late in 1917 and evolved from its biplane forerunner, the W-12. These seaplanes were used extensively for reconnaissance duties and to escort U-boats through the Allied minefields. The fuselage was constructed from plywood and nicknamed 'the coffin' as it resembled in shape and colour German and Austrian funeral caskets.

Fabric was used to cover the wings, which were heavily strutted to the marine ply-covered floats and fuselage, thus eliminating the need for rigging wires. The rudder was also fabric covered and inverted on the rear of the fuselage to provide an uninterrupted view for the rear gunner.

Modelling the W-29 is fairly straightforward, being mainly constructed from sheet balsa. The wings, tail-plane, and floats are carved from the solid, whilst the fuselage is built up using the box method.

20 Hansa Brandenberg W-29.

Materials

Fuselage 2.5mm ($\frac{3}{32}$in.), 1.5mm ($\frac{1}{16}$in.), and 0.8mm ($\frac{1}{32}$in.) sheet balsa.
Wings and floats, 6.0mm ($\frac{1}{4}$in.) sheet balsa.
Tail-plane and rudder, 1.5mm ($\frac{1}{16}$in.) sheet balsa.
Propeller, 3.0mm ($\frac{1}{8}$in.) sheet balsa.
Wing and floats struts, engine cylinders, 3.0mm ($\frac{1}{8}$in.) birch dowel.
Engine block, 6.0mm ($\frac{1}{4}$in.) sheet balsa.
Struts and wing lugs, 22 gauge piano-wire.
Exhausts and manifolds, 18 gauge brass wire.
Wing ribs and float battens, thread.
Windscreen, clear acetate sheet.
Control wires, 5 amp. fuse-wire.

Construction

Trace onto 1.5mm ($\frac{1}{16}$in.) sheet balsa from the plan the two fuselage sides, together with frames, (A), (B), (C), and (D), and cut them out. Mark the positions of the frames on the fuselage sides, bevel the inside rear edges of the fuselage sides where they meet at the rudder, and assemble them with glue. Take care that the frames are parallel to each other and the sides are level.

21 Gun-well marked ready for cutting out and shaping.

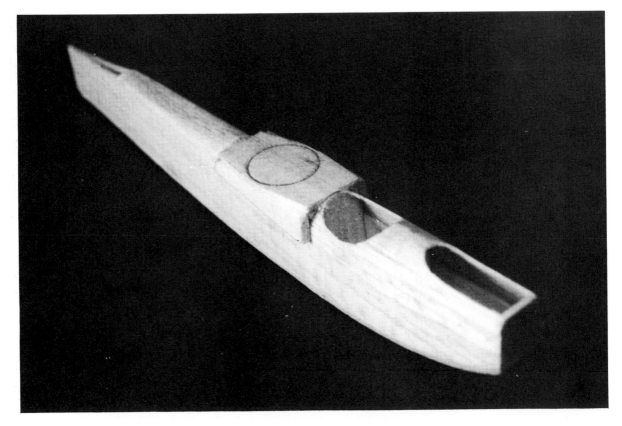

Trace and cut out the bottom from 1.5mm ($\frac{1}{16}$in.) sheet balsa. This is in two sections; the front section goes across the grain to facilitate bending and is glued in place first; this is followed by the rear section, with the grain running lengthways.

Use 0.8mm ($\frac{1}{32}$in.) sheet balsa for the fuselage top and trace and cut it from the plan in two main sections. In view of the curved front section it is advisable to make a paper template first before cutting the balsa to ensure a neat fit. Cut out the engine bay and cockpit and score them with a knife lengthways to facilitate bending them over the frames. The rear gunner's cockpit is cut out after gluing. Pin the sides in place while the glue is setting. Glue the rear top section to the fuselage sides and butting against the front section. Trim and smooth down as necessary.

The belled-out rear gunner's cockpit is made by tracing and cutting it out from 1.5mm ($\frac{1}{16}$in.) sheet balsa part (E); the middle is grooved out on the underside to fit on top of the fuselage. Cut out the sides (F) from 0.8mm ($\frac{1}{32}$in.) sheet balsa and glue under each side of (E) against the fuselage sides.

When set, cut out the cockpit and carve and sand it to shape. Trace and cut out the radiator from 2.5mm ($\frac{3}{32}$in.) sheet balsa and glue to the front of the fuselage.

Construct the engine block from 6.0mm ($\frac{1}{4}$in.) sheet balsa, traced from the plan. The cylinders are cut from 3.0mm ($\frac{1}{8}$in.) birch dowel and glued into pre-drilled holes in the top of the

22 Engine detail.

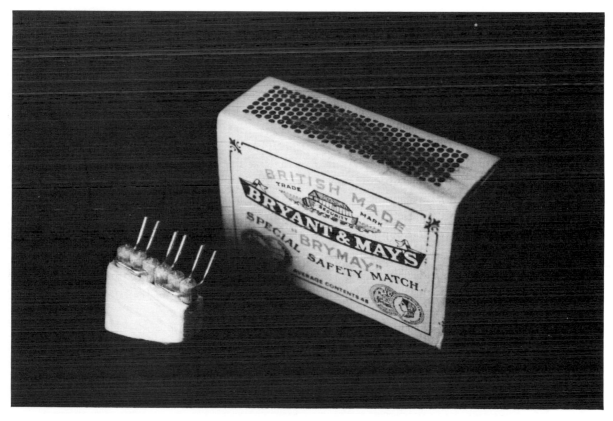

Hansa Brandenberg W-29

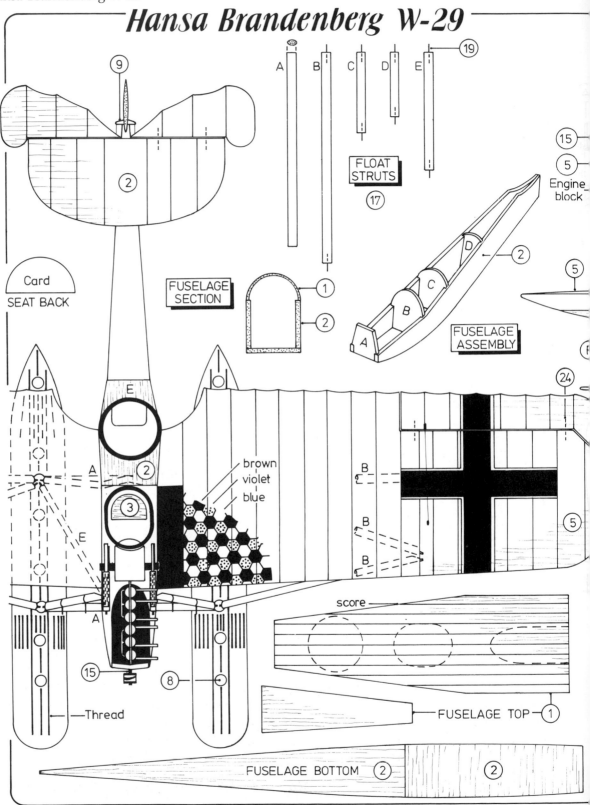

A B C D E

19

FLOAT STRUTS
17

15
5
Engine block

5

9

2

Card
SEAT BACK

FUSELAGE SECTION
1
2

FUSELAGE ASSEMBLY
A B C D
2

24

E
2

A
E
3

brown
violet
blue

B
B
B

5

A
15
Thread
8

score

FUSELAGE TOP 1

FUSELAGE BOTTOM 2   2

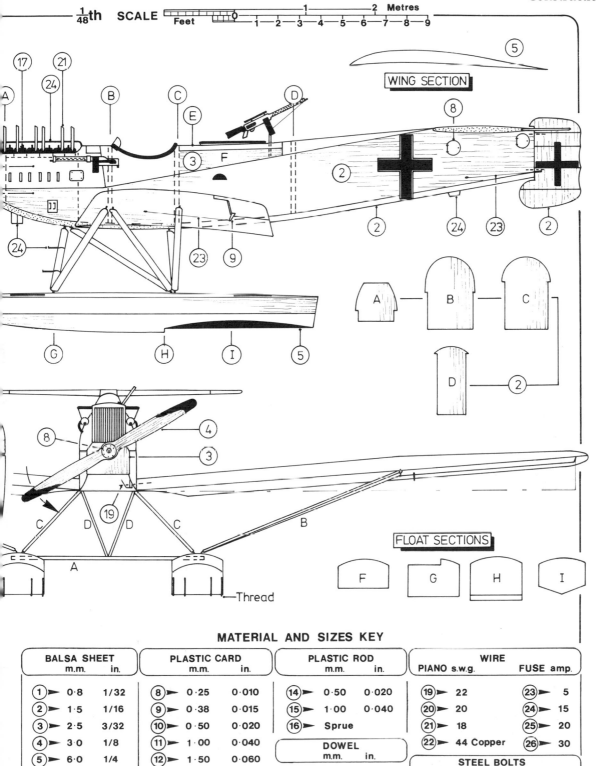

$\frac{1}{48}$th SCALE

Feet

Metres

WING SECTION

FLOAT SECTIONS

—Thread

MATERIAL AND SIZES KEY

BALSA SHEET m.m.	in.	PLASTIC CARD m.m.	in.	PLASTIC ROD m.m.	in.	WIRE PIANO s.w.g.	FUSE amp.
① ► 0·8	1/32	⑧ ► 0·25	0·010	⑭ ► 0·50	0·020	⑲ ► 22	㉓ ► 5
② ► 1·5	1/16	⑨ ► 0·38	0·015	⑮ ► 1·00	0·040	⑳ ► 20	㉔ ► 15
③ ► 2·5	3/32	⑩ ► 0·50	0·020	⑯ ► Sprue		㉑ ► 18	㉕ ► 20
④ ► 3·0	1/8	⑪ ► 1·00	0·040	DOWEL m.m.	in.	㉒ ► 44 Copper	㉖ ► 30
⑤ ► 6·0	1/4	⑫ ► 1·50	0·060	⑰ ► 3·0	1/8	STEEL BOLTS m.m.	in.
⑥ ► 9·0	3/8	⑬ ► 2·00	0·080	⑱ ► 9·0	3/8	㉗ ► 2·5	3/32
⑦ ► 25×25	1×1sq.						

engine block. Use 18g brass wire to make the manifolds and exhaust pipes; these are cut and bent to shape and epoxied into pre-drilled holes in the cylinder sides. Do not glue the engine in place until the painting is finished.

Trace and cut out the wings from 6.0mm ($\frac{1}{4}$in.) sheet balsa and also the tail-plane and rudder from 1.5mm ($\frac{1}{16}$in.) balsa. Shape the wings to an aerofoil section with undercamber and tapering from the strut locations to the tips. Mark and cut out the ailerons as these will be hinged with fuse-wire at appropriate angles after they have been painted. Similarly, cut the elevators seperately and shape the tail-plane and rudder.

Wing and tail-plane ribs are formed by gluing polyester thread on the top and bottom of the flying surfaces. I recommend P.V.A. glue for this, as shown in the chapter on techniques.

The floats are constructed from two layers of 6.0mm ($\frac{1}{4}$in.) sheet balsa, glued together to form the correct depth. Trace the profiles of the floats, including the top of the deck cambers, and cut out. Next trace the plan shapes, carve as shown and smooth down. The battens and foot runs are made from thread, marked, and then fixed with P.V.A. glue.

Shape the wing and float struts to an oval section from 3.0mm ($\frac{1}{8}$in.) birch dowel and cut into appropriate lengths and numbers as shown on the plan marked (A) to (E). Only struts (B) to (E) are

23 Parts ready for assembly.

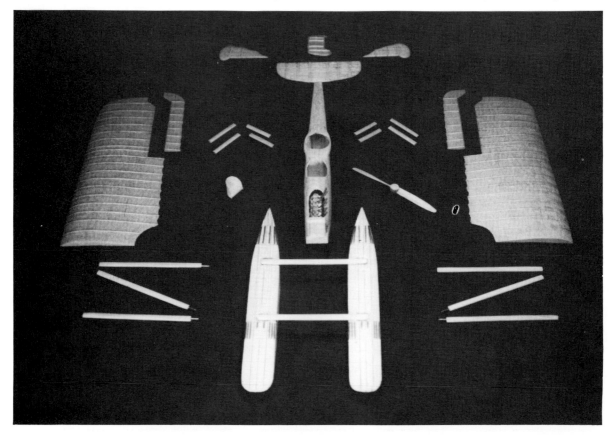

fitted with 22g piano-wire attachment lugs, inserted through pre-drilled holes in the ends of the struts. Struts (A) are glued into cut-outs in the tops of the floats to link them together.

Mark the position of the wing roots on the sides of the fuselage and bevel the roots to give the wings the correct dihedral. Cut four wing lugs out of 22g piano-wire and insert two in each wing root through pre-drilled holes, and glue and push wings into position with the lugs piercing the sides of the fuselage. Support the wing tips with pieces of balsa with the fuselage flat on the table until the glue has set.

Drill holes for the piano-wire strut lugs in float cross-members (A), and the fuselage and wings. Epoxy struts (C) and (D) into the flat cross-members; solder the lugs together at the top where they meet at the fuselage and epoxy through the holes. Epoxy the remaining wing struts (B) and float struts (E) into position. It may be necessary to bend and trim the locating lugs first to help align them.

Trace and carve the propeller from 3.0mm ($\frac{1}{8}$in.) sheet balsa and smooth down to an aerofoil section and pitch for an anti-clockwise rotation. The bucket seat base is traced and cut from 2.5mm ($\frac{3}{32}$in.) sheet balsa, and thin card is cut out for the back and glued around the edge of the seat.

Finishing

Smooth down the fuselage and floats with fine glasspaper. Only smooth the edges of the flying surfaces where the thread ribs end. Apply two coats of sanding sealer to cover the entire model, including inside the engine bay, cockpit, and gun-well. Lightly smooth down and repeat with further coats as necessary to seal the grain and the thread ribs.

Trace, using a pencil, hexagonal camouflage outlines from the plan onto sheets of thin model aeroplane tissue, which are cut a little larger than the surfaces to be covered. Dope the marked tissue onto the upper surfaces of the wings and tail-plane, including the ailerons and elevators. Also cover the top of the fuselage between the gun-well and tail-plane. Use clear cellulose dope and dab it on with a brush through the tissue, making sure not to trap any air bubbles. Trim the edges of the tissue when dry and apply a further coat of clear dope to seal the edges; fill any remaining open weave in the tissue.

Paint on the blue-grey base colour of the camouflage using thinned enamel. Next paint in the violet and brown hexagonal pattern. To simplify this lengthy process cut out a hexagonal stencil from a rubber and apply a coat of paint to the stencil, transferring it to model by light pressure until the pattern is complete.

Paint the remainder of the fuselage with blue-grey enamel. The rudder and cockpit interior is white, and the underside of the flying surfaces is natural linen colour. Floats, seat, struts, and cockpit padding are painted brown. The engine block is silver with dark grey cylinders and copper coloured piping. When it is dry, glue the engine into the fuselage and attach

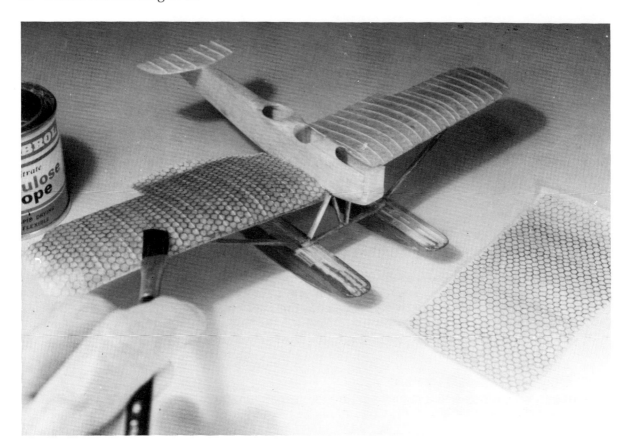

remaining piping, which is grey. Also paint grey the rear fuselage hatches, handles, steps, propeller boss, and control horns.
All these items are made from scrap plastic card and wire and
glued in position.

The machine guns (which were obtained commercially) are
also painted grey and glued to the fuselage sides where shown.
Mount the rear facing gun into a short length of brass tubing,
pushed into a pre-drilled hole in the rear of the gun well. This
will permit the gun to be pivoted in any position.

Attach the rudder, ailerons, and elevators with fuse-wire and
bend them to the required position. Apply the transfer insignia
markings. Mark panel lines on the fuselage with pencil, using a
straight edge as a guide. Coat the entire model with semi-matt
clear varnish, including the propeller, which should first be
stained with mahogany dye.

Cut to length the control wires from 5 amp. fuse-wire and
glue into position, including the acetate windscreen. Paint the
radiator and also the propeller-tips brass. Line in the radiator
grills with a ruling pen and mark on hatch hinges etc. Fasten the
propeller with the boss onto a length of plastic rod shaft, glued
into a pre-drilled hole below the radiator. Cockpit details such as
the control column, throttle lever, priming pump and instrument dials, are made from scrap wire and plastic card, and
glued in position.

24 Doping on the camouflage-
marked tissue.

nine
Junkers D1

Introduction

The Junkers D1, with its low monoplane configuration, probably heralded the beginning of the modern aeroplane as we know it today. Designed by Professor Hugo Junkers, the aircraft had an exceptionally thick aerofoil cantilevered wing, thus dispensing with the usual external bracing. The other unusual feature, which was revolutionary at the time, was that the entire airframe was covered in a corrugated metal skin, and, owing to its success, it remained characteristic of nearly all Junkers aeroplanes until the mid-thirties.

The engine layout is similar to the Hansa Brandenburg, with its automotive-type, front-mounted radiator. Early machines were powered by a 160 h.p. Mercedes engine, but were later replaced by the more powerful 185 h.p. Benz engine, which gave a top speed of around 193.1kmh (120 mph).

Little is known about the battle record of these aircraft as they did not enter service until almost the end of the hostilities. However, captured examples after Armistice showed that they were resistant to battle damage and could withstand exposure when left out in the open.

25 Junkers D1.

Reproducing the corrugated skin effect on the model is achieved by scoring grooves, close and parallel to one another, on plastic card before the parts are cut out. Plastic card is used almost entirely throughout the model, including for the engine, which is made from plastic rod and sprue. Sheet balsa is used for the propeller and wing cores.

Materials

Fuselage, 0.38mm (0.015in.), and 0.50mm (0.020in.), plastic card.
Tail-plane and rudder, 0.38mm (0.015in.) plastic card.
Wings, 0.25mm (0.010in.) plastic card.
Wing cores, 6.00mm ($\frac{1}{4}$in.) sheet balsa.
Radiator and tail-skid, 1.00mm (0.040in.) plastic card.
Engine cylinders, 3.0mm ($\frac{1}{8}$in.) plastic rod.
Undercarriage struts, exhaust, and axle, 1.00mm (0.040in.) plastic rod.
Undercarriage bracing and exhaust stubs, 0.50mm (0.020in.) plastic rod.
Windscreen fairing, axle, and engine fairings, 0.25mm (0.010in.) plastic card.
Wheels, 1.00mm (0.040in.), and 0.50mm (0.020in.) plastic card.
Wheel covers, 0.38mm (0.015in.) moulded plastic card.
Seat, 0.50mm (0.020in.), and 0.25mm (0.010in.) plastic card.
Propeller, 3.00mm ($\frac{1}{8}$in.) sheet balsa.
Windscreen, clear acetate sheet.
Crash bar, 0.50mm (0.020in.) plastic rod, and sprue.

Construction

Before cutting out and assembly can begin, the first job is to make the corrugated effect on the plastic card. Cut out enough card for the fuselage and flying surfaces and using a small screwdriver score parallel grooves close to one another. A tee square is ideal for ensuring the grooves are parallel. Any good straight edge, however, would do. The card should be taped to the work surface and re-taped as the scoring progresses, owing to some distortion that will occur.

Trace and cut out from the corrugated 0.38mm (0.015in.) plastic card the fuselage sides and top and bottom sections. These sections should be cut slightly over size to allow for fitting. Also trace and cut out from 0.50mm (0.020in.) plastic card frames (A), (B), (C), and (D) and the radiator.

Mark the positions of frames (B), (C), and (D) on the fuselage sides and assemble, holding the frames in place with Blu-Tack. Ensure that the sides are level and glue all the frames, including frame (A), and the rear of the fuselage together. Glue the front bottom section to the underside of the fuselage, followed by the rear section, and hold in place with tape until it has set.

Cut out 3mm wide strips from 1.00mm (0.040in.) plastic card and glue them along the top of the fuselage sides, between the

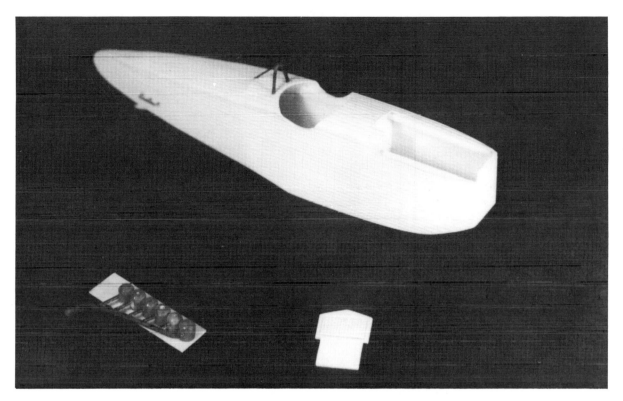

frames. These will straighten out any bumps in the sides and also provide a base for gluing the curved top. Glue the top front section in place first followed by the rear section, and hold in place with tape until set. Cut out the apertures for the cockpit and engine bay. The 3mm wide strengthener strips will also need to be cut away. Replace the strips on each side of the cockpit, glued to the fuselage sides.

Cut out and shape the six engine cylinders from 3.00mm ($\frac{1}{8}$in.) plastic rod, glue to a suitable base made from plastic card and cut them to fit between frame (A) and (B). Bend and shape the exhaust pipe from 1.00mm (0.040in.) plastic rod and glue to the ends of the 0.50mm (0.020in.) exhaust stubs, which in turn are glued to the cylinders. Cut from 0.50mm (0.020in.) plastic rod the six valves and glue into pre-drilled holes in the top of the cylinders. Glue the engine in the bay, together with the radiator and side panels, cut from 0.38mm (0.015in.) corrugated plastic card.

To complete the fuselage, shape and glue the tail-skid in position, together with the crash bar made from plastic rod as specified. Cut out from corrugated 0.25mm (0.010in.) plastic card the two engine vents and glue to each side of the fuselage. Cut and bend the pilot step, port side only, and the lifting handles from sprue or plastic rod and glue in place.

Trace and cut out from corrugated 0.38mm (0.015in.) plastic card both halves of the tail-plane and rudder. Insert a piece of same thickness plastic card as shown on the plan between the two halves of the tail-plane before gluing together to form an

26 Fuselage and engine block assemblies.

Junkers D1.

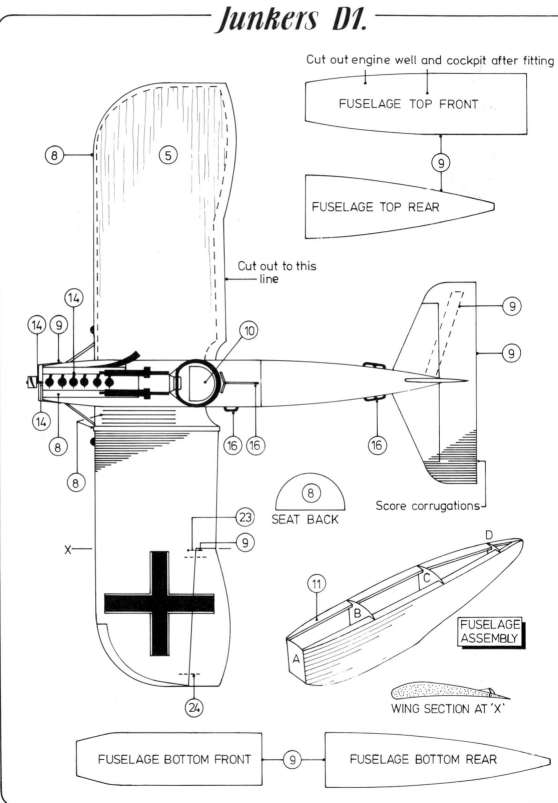

Cut out engine well and cockpit after fitting

FUSELAGE TOP FRONT

FUSELAGE TOP REAR

8   5

Cut out to this line

14

14 9

10

14

8

8

16 16

16

9

9

Score corrugations

8
SEAT BACK

23

9

X

24

11

B

C

D

A

FUSELAGE ASSEMBLY

WING SECTION AT 'X'

FUSELAGE BOTTOM FRONT   9   FUSELAGE BOTTOM REAR

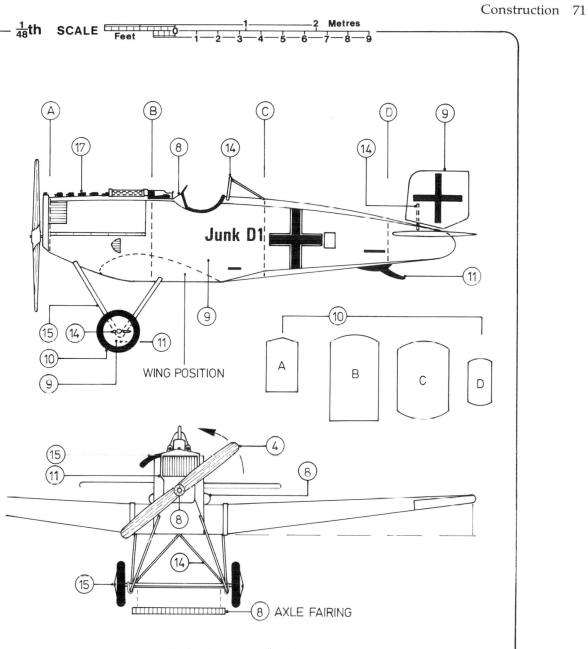

1/48th SCALE

Junk D1

WING POSITION

AXLE FAIRING

MATERIAL AND SIZES KEY

BALSA SHEET m.m.	in.	PLASTIC CARD m.m.	in.	PLASTIC ROD m.m.	in.	WIRE PIANO s.w.g.	FUSE amp.
(1) 0·8	1/32	(8) 0·25	0·010	(14) 0·50	0·020	(19) 22	(23) 5
(2) 1·5	1/16	(9) 0·38	0·015	(15) 1·00	0·040	(20) 20	(24) 15
(3) 2·5	3/32	(10) 0·50	0·020	(16) Sprue		(21) 18	(25) 20
(4) 3·0	1/8	(11) 1·00	0·040	DOWEL m.m.	in.	(22) 44 Copper	(26) 30
(5) 6·0	1/4	(12) 1·50	0·060	(17) 3·0	1/8	STEEL BOLTS m.m.	in.
(6) 9·0	3/8	(13) 2·00	0·080	(18) 9·0	3/8	(27) 2·5	3/32
(7) 25×25	1×1sq.						

aerofoil section. When set, smooth edges and score the elevator hinge. Cut the right angled ends and bend the elevator to the required position before gluing to the fuselage.

For the rudder, cut a suitable length of 0.50mm (0.020in.) plastic rod and glue it between the rudder halves to form the pivot. Smooth edges and insert the rudder into a pre-drilled hole in the fuselage where shown.

Construct the wings, which you have traced and cut out from corrugated 0.25mm (0.010in.) plastic card, by folding them round a 6.0mm ($\frac{1}{4}$in.) sheet balsa core. Cut away the centre section and partially cut through each wing root from the top and glue to the correct dihedral, as shown on the plan. Cut thin strips of 0.25mm (0.010in.) plastic card for the wing root join bands and foot runs, and glue in place. Mark and cut out the ailerons and smooth and seal exposed edges with polystyrene cement. Seal the end grain of the balsa core on each wing root with cement and glue the wing to the fuselage sides in the position shown. Prop up each wing tip while the glue is setting.

Bend and cut to length the two undercarriage vee struts from 1.00mm (0.040in.) plastic rod and file to an aerofoil section. Mark and drill the strut positions in the wing and fuselage and glue in place. The rear struts should be vertical. Cut to length the axle and centre bracing from plastic rod as specified and glue in position. Cut out the rear cross bracing fairing from two strips

27 Model ready for painting and detailing.

of corrugated 0.25mm (0.010in.) plastic card. Glue the two halves together and glue between the vee struts behind the axle. Construct the wheels from plastic card as specified using the method described in the chapter on techniques.

Finally, trace and cut out the propeller from 3.0mm ($\frac{1}{8}$in.) sheet balsa and smooth to shape. The propeller shaft is cut from 0.50mm (0.020in.) plastic rod and glued into a pre-drilled hole in the radiator. Roll out plastic filler for the cockpit padding and glue in place together with the windscreen fairing cut from 0.25mm (0.010in.) plastic card. The windscreen itself is fitted after the painting is finished, together with the pilot seat which is made from plastic card as specified.

Finishing

Paint the underside of the fuselage, wings, tail-plane, rudder, wheel covers, and undercarriage struts white. Also paint white the rear part of the sides and top of the fuselage.

The upper surfaces of the wings are pale green, with irregular patches of light mauve painted on top. The ailerons should be attached to the wings with 15 amp. fuse wire before painting the wings so that the mauve camouflage effect will match.

Paint the inside of the engine bay matt black and the cockpit pale matt green. The fuselage top and sides are chocolate

28 Cockpit and gun mountings (note firing button on control column).

brown, including the upper tail-plane surfaces. The cockpit padding is tan coloured, and light or dark grey is applied where appropriate to the handles, step, engine cylinders, radiator, crash bar, tail-skid, tyres, axle, and propeller boss.

Apply the cross insignia transfers and panel lines with a ruling pen. Dry transfer sheets are used for the wording on the side of the fuselage. Coat the entire model with clear matt varnish.

Paint the machine guns dark grey and also the exhaust pipes, which are tinged with copper. Glue the machine guns in place, together with the radiator cap, cut from plastic rod and painted brass coloured. Stain and varnish the propeller and fasten with the propeller boss.

Cut out the control horns from scrap plastic card and glue to the upper surfaces only of the ailerons. Glue short lengths of 5 amp. fuse-wire between the control horns and wings and paint grey.

Construct the cockpit details from scrap plastic card, sprue and fuse-wire. The fittings include the control column, throttle lever, primer pump and instrument panel suitably painted and detailed. Paint the seat matt brown and glue it to a piece of balsa packing so that the seat is at the correct height in the cockpit, and glue in place. Cut out the windscreen from clear acetate sheet and glue to the inside of the fairing. The pilot was obtained commercially (as were the Spandau machine guns) and suitably painted and held in his seat with Blu-Tack.

Nieuport II Bèbè constructed from plastic card with bought white metal engine and figures, suitably painted.

Morane Saulnier showing stretched plastic sprue wing warping control wires and rotary engine constructed from cut down bolts.

Albatross DIII with stained and varnished balsa wood carved fuselage complements its full size counterpart, while plastic card is used for constructing the wings and tail plane.

Hansa Brandenberg W-29 flying boat constructed from balsa wood with hand painted hexagonal camouflage markings.

ten

De Havilland DH2

Introduction

Designed in the spring of 1915 as a fighting scout, the DH2 had a pusher layout, the engine being mounted behind the pilot to overcome the problem of synchronizing the Lewis 303in. machine gun, which would be necessary with a conventional tractor arrangement. The pusher layout did, however, have two disadvantages. Firstly, owing to the drag effect of the tail booms, its speed was disappointing even in a prolonged dive. To try and overcome this the cylinders of the rotary engines were bored out to achieve more power, but on earlier machines this weakened the engine crankcase, resulting in one or more of its nine cylinders parting company and severing the tail booms. Secondly, with the exposed cockpit being some distance forward from the engine, pilots suffered from the cold. Indeed, at least one pilot lost his life owing to his legs numbing and the aircraft consequently spinning out of control into the ground.

The fuselage, wings, and tail-plane were fabric-covered on a wooden framework, with the tail-plane supported on four wire braced, tubular-steel booms.

Balsa wood forms the main structure for the model, the wings and tail-plane. Piano-wire is used for tail-boom, undercarriage, and wing struts to strengthen this frail-looking aircraft.

29 De Havilland DH2.

Materials

Fuselage, 6mm ($\frac{1}{4}$in.), 1.5mm ($\frac{1}{16}$in.), and 0.8mm ($\frac{1}{32}$in.) sheet
  balsa.
Tail-plane and fin, 1.5mm ($\frac{1}{16}$in.) sheet balsa.
Tail-booms and wheel-axle, 20 gauge piano-wire.
Wing struts and undercarriage, 22 gauge piano-wire.
Propeller and wings, 3.0mm ($\frac{1}{8}$in.) sheet balsa.
Wing strut fairings and tail-boom bracing, 0.8mm ($\frac{1}{32}$in.) sheet
  balsa.
Fuel tank, 3.0mm ($\frac{1}{8}$in.) birch dowel.
Wheels, plastic card and filler.
Controls and rigging wire, 5 amp. fuse-wire.

Construction

The fuselage is built up on the box method of construction and
consists of a flat bottom and sides, supported by three frames on
top of which the curved top deck is formed. Balsa block or sheet
is used for carving the nacelle.
  Start by tracing and cutting out from 1.5mm ($\frac{1}{16}$in.) sheet
balsa: the fuselage bottom, sides and the three frames (2 No. (A)
and one (B)). Mark the positions of the frames onto the fuselage
sides and glue the two sides squarely to the frames. Glue the

30 Parts ready for assembly
    (note piano-wire wing lugs).

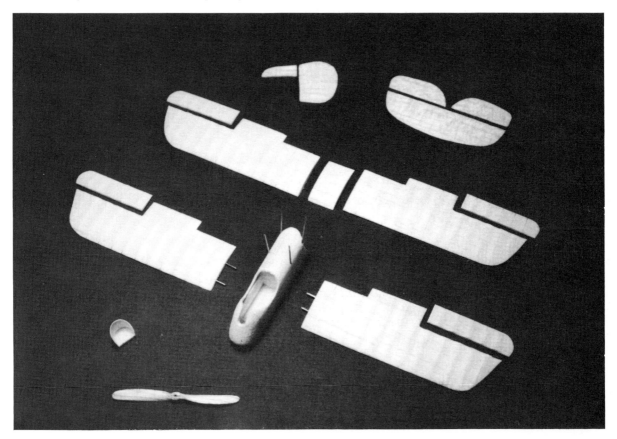

bottom to the bottom of the frames and fuselage sides. Make a paper template of the curved top deck first before cutting it out of 0.8mm ($\frac{1}{32}$in.) sheet balsa to ensure a good fit. Bend the balsa deck in water and dry over a heat source before gluing it over the frames, otherwise it may crack. Trace and cut out from 0.8mm ($\frac{1}{32}$in.) sheet balsa the two cockpit corners (C) and glue in place. Cut the nacelle from two layers of 6.0mm ($\frac{1}{4}$in.) sheet balsa, laminated together along the centre line. Glue to the front of frame (B) and when set carve to shape. Cut out the gun position in the top and hollow out the inside of the nacelle, including frame (B). Smooth down as far as possible and coat the inside with balsa cement to seal the grain. Fair in the edges of the sides, top and the nacelle, and smooth down with fine glasspaper.

Trace and cut out from 3.0mm ($\frac{1}{8}$in.) sheet balsa the top and lower wings. The top wing is cut out complete from tip to tip and shaped to an aerofoil section before you cut out the centre section. The lower wing is also cut this way, except there is no centre section to cut out. Mark the positions of the ribs on the upper surfaces and, with a half round file, shape shallow grooves out between the ribs. Mark the positions of the ailerons and cut out and smooth round the leading edges.

Bevel the wing roots of the top wings and glue to the centre section over the plan to obtain the correct dihedral. Also bevel the lower wing roots and insert two 22g. piano-wire lugs, cut to about 9mm ($\frac{3}{8}$in.) long in each wing. Mark the positions of the lower wings on the sides of the fuselage and glue and push the protruding wing lugs into the sides, holding the completed top wing underneath as a guide to obtain the same dihedral until the glue has set.

Mark the positions of the wing struts from the plan and drill through both upper and lower wings. Also mark and drill through the fuselage top deck for the four centre section struts. Cut eight 22g. wing struts to length and four shorter centre wing struts from the plan. Insert struts into the upper surface of the lower wing, including the centre section into the top of the fuselage, and locate the upper wing on top of all the struts. When all the struts are located in their respective holes and the wings are level, with no stagger, apply glue to the struts and leave to set.

Cut and bend to the angle shown on the plan the 20g. piano-wire, lower booms, together with the two seperate top booms. Solder the ends of the lower booms to each of the two rear, inboard struts where they enter the lower wings at the angle shown on the plan. Cut to length the 22g. piano-wire tail-post and solder vertically on the inside rear corner of the lower booms.

Trace and cut out from 1.5mm ($\frac{1}{16}$in.) sheet balsa the tail-plane and fin, and reproduce the ribs using the same method as with the wings. Cut the elevators from the tail-plane and smooth round the leading edges, as these will be hinged with the ailerons after the painting is finished.

Mark the positions of the two upper booms where they enter

De Havilland DH 2

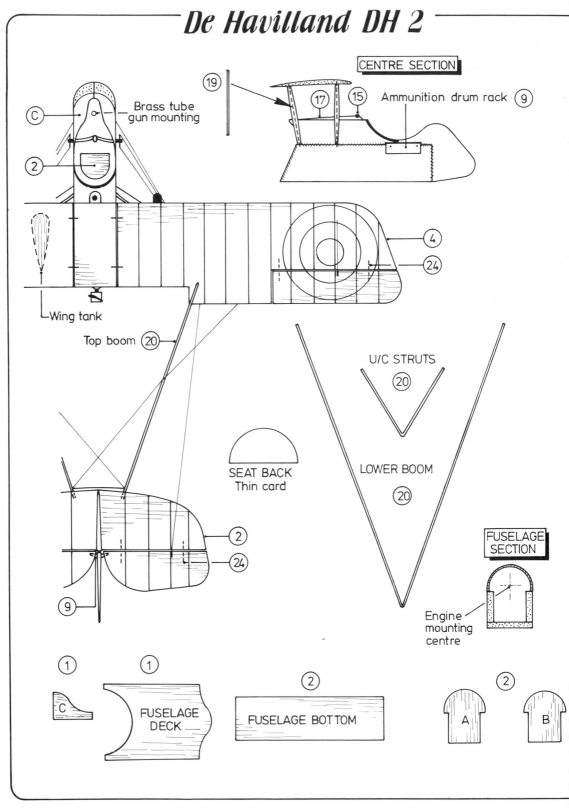

CENTRE SECTION

(19)

(17)   (15)   Ammunition drum rack (9)

C   Brass tube gun mounting

(2)

(4)

(24)

Wing tank

Top boom (20)

U/C STRUTS
(20)

SEAT BACK
Thin card

LOWER BOOM
(20)

(2)

(24)

FUSELAGE
SECTION

(9)

Engine
mounting
centre

(1)   (1)

C

FUSELAGE
DECK

(2)

FUSELAGE BOTTOM

(2)

A   B

$\frac{1}{48}$th **SCALE**

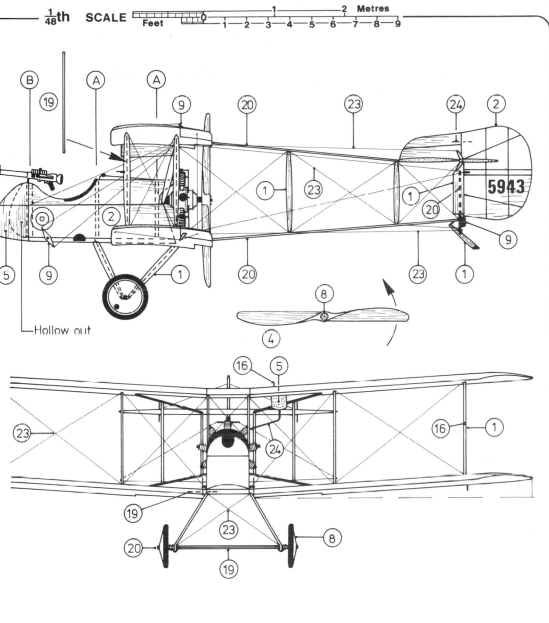

—Hollow out

5943

MATERIAL AND SIZES KEY

BALSA SHEET			PLASTIC CARD			PLASTIC ROD			WIRE			
	m.m.	in.		m.m.	in.		m.m.	in.	PIANO s.w.g.		FUSE amp.	
①►	0·8	1/32	⑧►	0·25	0·010	⑭►	0·50	0·020	⑲►	22	㉓►	5
②►	1·5	1/16	⑨►	0·38	0·015	⑮►	1·00	0·040	⑳►	20	㉔►	15
③►	2·5	3/32	⑩►	0·50	0·020	⑯►	Sprue		㉑►	18	㉕►	20
④►	3·0	1/8	⑪►	1·00	0·040	**DOWEL**			㉒►	44 Copper	㉖►	30
⑤►	6·0	1/4	⑫►	1·50	0·060		m.m.	in.	**STEEL BOLTS**			
⑥►	9·0	3/8	⑬►	2·00	0·080	⑰►	3·0	1/8		m.m.		in.
⑦►	25×25	1×1sq.				⑱►	9·0	3/8	㉗►	2·5		3/32

the upper wings and tail-plane. File the rear ends of booms to a
point and press them into the leading edge of the tail-plane.
Insert the front ends of the booms into pre-drilled holes in the
upper wings. Press the top of the tail-post into the centre of the
trailing edge of the tail-plane. When the assembly is aligned
correctly apply epoxy glue to the upper boom attachment points
and top of the tail-post.

Construct the undercarriage from two vee struts, cut and bent
as shown from 22g. piano-wire, and inserted through pre-
drilled holes in the fuselage in the position shown. Cut the
wheel axle from 20g. piano-wire and solder to each inside corner
of the vee struts. The suspension supports are made from 22g.
piano-wire and glued on each side of the axle. Epoxy the vee
struts to the fuselage after checking that the axle is aligned and
level.

Cut to length and shape the wing struts and undercarriage
fairings from 0.8mm ($\frac{1}{32}$in.) sheet balsa and saw a groove along
the centres so that they can be glued flush over the piano-wire
struts and undercarriage. Similarly cut out the tail-post from
0.8mm ($\frac{1}{32}$in.) sheet balsa and glue over the piano-wire. Mark
the positions of the bracing on the tail-booms and cut out and
glue between the upper and lower booms.

The tail-skid is cut from 0.8mm ($\frac{1}{32}$in.) sheet balsa and epoxied
to the bottom of the 22g. piano-wire tail-post. Glue the front
section of the fin centrally on top of the tail-plane. Construct the
top of the fuel tank from 3.0mm ($\frac{1}{8}$in.) birch dowel with the base
filed down at an angle and glued on top of the fuselage behind
the cockpit. Carve the propeller from 3.0mm ($\frac{1}{8}$in.) sheet balsa
and finally construct the wheels from plastic card and filler. The
rotary engine and machine gun are obtained commercially and
fitted after painting.

31 Lower wings glued at the
correct dihedral.

Finishing

Early aircraft were finished in clear dope applied to the flying surfaces with natural plywood on the nose and upper fuselage panels. The aircraft represented here is one of the first production batch and is finished accordingly. Later machines had all upper surfaces doped in khaki colour and were fitted with four-bladed propellers, with their tips sheathed in brass for protection against splitting due to debris being sucked up on take off.

Smooth down the entire model with fine glasspaper, paying particular attention to the scalloped-out rib detail on the flying surfaces and also the wing and boom struts. An emery board is suitable for this. Apply two coats of sanding sealer to all the balsa wood structure, including the inside of the cockpit. The control surfaces are treated seperately. Smooth down and repeat with a further coat of sanding sealer as necessary until there is no exposed grain.

Attach the ailerons to the wings with 15 amp. fuse-wire. The elevators and rudder are glued directly to the tail-plane at the required angle after painting. Cut out the control horns from thin plastic card and glue them into pre-cut slots. Cut out the footstep in the port side only of the fuselage and seal the exposed grain with polystyrene cement.

Apply two coats of natural linen colour (beige) to both sides of the flying surfaces and lower fuselage panels. The upper fuselage, nose, fin and undercarriage struts are dark brown. Paint the rudder with equal width vertical stripes of red, white and blue. All the wing and boom struts, including the cockpit padding and tail-skid, are tan coloured. The tail booms, engine cylinders, Lewis gun and other metal fittings are dark matt grey. Paint the wheel-centres red with light grey tyres.

Some further minor fittings will need to be constructed and painted; these include the wing gravity tank made from balsa sheet, sealed and painted grey, with the feed pipe made from 15 amp. fuse-wire and painted copper coloured. The pitot tube, elevator control crank, and tail-skid, steering-control horn, are made from scrap plastic card and rod, painted grey and glued in position.

Apply the roundel transfers and serial numbers. Mark on the stitching and rib positions on the underside of the flying surfaces with a pencil. Also use a pencil for general shading and weathering effect. Coat the entire model with semi-gloss clear varnish except the cockpit padding and wheels, which are varnished with matt.

Mount the machine-gun in a suitable length of brass tube, glued to the cockpit bottom. Cut a short length of plastic rod for the fuel cap, glue it to the top of the fuel tank and paint it grey. Install the engine and propeller assembly complete with the propeller boss, cut from thin-painted, grey plastic card, to the rear of the fuselage through a pre-drilled hole and glue it in. Brass tube is inserted over the engine shaft and retained with a blob of glue before fitting if you want the engine to rotate.

Cut to length the rigging from 5 amp. fuse-wire and glue them in place, starting at the centre section and finishing with the

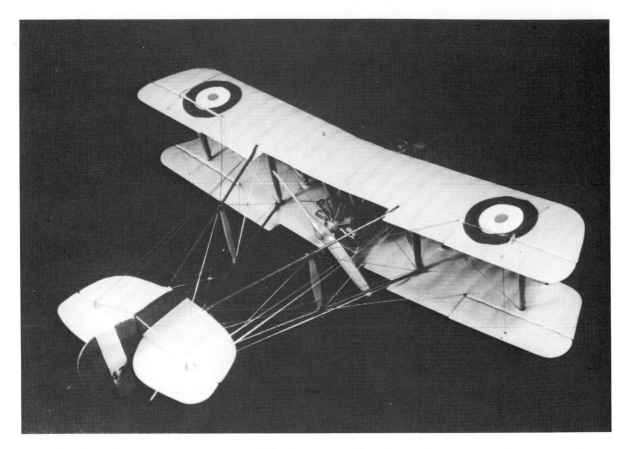

control wires. The cross-over points of the flying and landing wires are clipped together on the full sized aircraft; these are represented on the model by blobs of glue painted grey. Other details such as the balance springs on the top ailerons are picked out with a ruling pen and ink. Use a pen to show strut fastening brackets and rigging and control fastenings.

A white metal pilot obtained commercially was used. The legs were reshaped using a file to enable him to sit correctly in the cockpit and then suitably painted. The seat is omitted if you choose to have a pilot, owing to lack of space.

32 Rear view showing pusher arrangement.

eleven

Nieuport 11 Bèbè

Introduction

With a wing span of only 7.55m (24ft 9¼in.) and length of 5.80m (19ft ½in.), the aircraft was nicknamed the Bèbè by the French pilots. The 80 h.p. nine cylinder Le Rhône rotary engine gave a top speed of 156kmh (96.8mph). Armament was a single Lewis 303in. machine gun, mounted to a bracket on the upper wing in order to clear the arc of the propeller. The ailerons were operated by pear-shaped cranks in the centre wing section, from which rods were connected vertically down through the deck to the control column in the cockpit. The Bèbè entered service in the summer of 1915 and proved to be so successful a match for the Fokker fighters that the Germans ordered copies to be made.

Plastic card is used throughout in modelling the Bèbè, with the exception of the engine, propeller, and machine gun, which are white metal fittings obtained commercially.

33 Niewport 11 Bèbè.

Materials

Fuselage, 0.50mm (0.020in.), and 0.25mm (0.010in.) plastic
  card.
Cowling, 1.00mm (0.040in.), 0.50mm (0.020in.), and
  0.25mm (0.010in.) plastic card.
Wings, tail-plane and rudder, 0.25mm (0.010in.) plastic card.
Wing cores, 1.5mm ($\frac{1}{16}$in.) sheet balsa.
Wing and tail-plane struts, 0.25mm (0.010in.) plastic card.
Undercarriage struts and axle, 1.00mm (0.040in.) plastic rod.
Wheels, 1.00mm (0.040in.), and 0.50mm (0.020in.) plastic card.
Wheel covers, 0.25mm (0.010in.), moulded plastic card.
Seat, 1.00mm (0.040in.), and 0.25mm (0.010in.) plastic card.
Tail-skid and aileron cranks, plastic sprue.
Control and rigging wires, stretched plastic sprue or 5 amp.
  fuse-wire.

Construction

Trace and cut out from 0.50mm (0.020in.) plastic card, frames
(A), (B), and (C), together with the fuselage sides and bottom.
Mark the position of frame (C) on the fuselage sides and glue in
place, together with frame (B). Bring together the pointed rear
end of the fuselage and glue, checking that all the frames and
sides are square and level. Glue the bottom in place and trim
edges, if necessary, when set.

Trace and cut out the fuselage top from 0.25mm (0.010in.)
plastic card, but not the cockpit opening. Tear off thin strips of
masking tape and secure top to the fuselage sides. Lightly glue
between the tape, which is then removed when set, and apply
more glue if necessary when the tapes have been removed.

Construct the cowling around frame (A) from plastic card as
specified, and glue to the front of the fuselage. Trace and cut out
the rear cowling cheeks, together with the access panels,
breather-pipe flanges, and windscreen sides from 0.25mm
(0.010in.) plastic card. Fastening screws in the access panels are
represented by pressing a blunt pencil point in the reverse sides,
which will show as small bumps on the outside.

Cut out the cockpit opening and trace and cut out the windscreen frame and tail-skid fairing from 1.00mm (0.040in.) plastic
card. These items, together with the other fuselage fittings, can
now be glued in place.

The wings, tail-plane and rudder are constructed in two
halves from 0.25mm (0.010in.) plastic card, traced and cut out
from the plan as shown. The ribbing effect is scored on the
insides using the method described in the chapter on techniques. Only the wings have balsa cores. The tail-plane and
rudder halves are glued directly together. Cut out the ailerons in
the upper wing as shown and also cut away the elevators from
the tail-plane. Cut out the control horns from 0.38mm (0.015in.)
plastic card and glue to both surfaces of the rudder and elevators
in the positions shown. Mark the positions of the two aileron
cranks from the plan on both surfaces of the upper wing. The
cranks are made by bending plastic sprue, cut to length and
glued in place.

Bend and cut the two undercarriage vee struts from 1.00mm (0.040in.) plastic rod and file down to an oval section. Glue each vee strut to the underside of the fuselage through pre-drilled holes in the position shown. Cut the axle from the same size plastic rod to length and glue to the inside apexes of each strut.

Construct the wheels from plastic card as specified and shape. Glue the wheel-covers, moulded from 0.25mm (0.010in.) plastic card, to the outer wheel-faces and drill through for the axle.

Trace and cut out from 0.50mm (0.020in.) plastic card the two outer wing vee struts and the four centre section struts. Glue the centre section struts to the fuselage where shown. The rear struts are glued together to form an inverted vee.

Glue the lower wings to the fuselage sides in the position shown. Locate the upper wing on top of the centre section struts and cut slots in the underside of the wing to receive the struts. Check that the wings are in correct alignment and glue in position. If necessary trim to length the two outer vee struts and glue them between the upper and lower wings. Glue the tail-plane to the rear of the fuselage, with the leading edge butting up against the top deck. Cut the two tail-plane struts from 0.25mm (0.010in.) plastic card and glue them between the rear of the tail-skid fairing and the tail-plane.

The cockpit padding is formed by rolling Blu-Tack into a thin length and lightly pressed around the cockpit rim. Thin down some polystyrene cement with solvent and brush onto the Blu-Tack. This will bond the padding to the fuselage and, when set hard, will provide a base for painting on.

Finally, construct the seat from plastic card, as specified, and the machine gun bracket from plastic sprue.

34 Parts ready for painting and assembly.

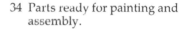

Nieuport 11 Bèbè

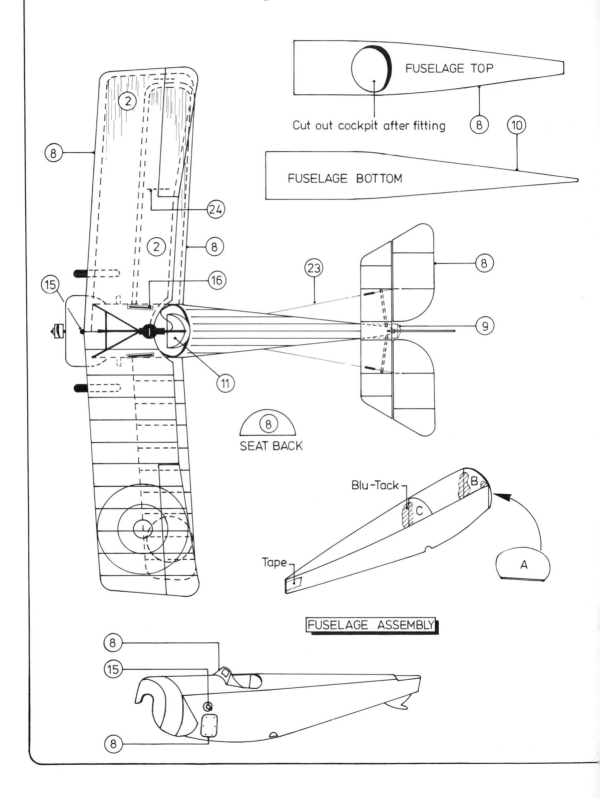

FUSELAGE TOP

Cut out cockpit after fitting

FUSELAGE BOTTOM

SEAT BACK

Blu-Tack

Tape

FUSELAGE ASSEMBLY

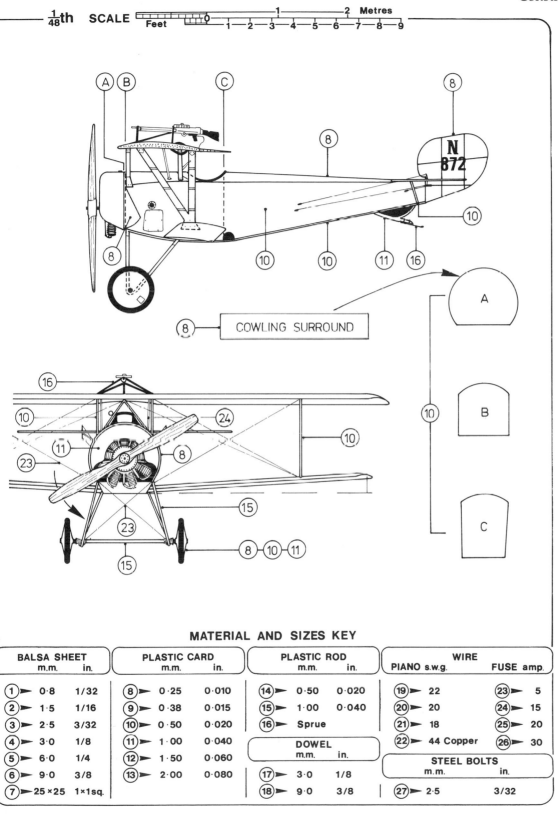

$\frac{1}{48}$th SCALE   Metres · Feet

COWLING SURROUND

MATERIAL AND SIZES KEY

BALSA SHEET		PLASTIC CARD		PLASTIC ROD		WIRE			
m.m.	in.	m.m.	in.	m.m.	in.	PIANO s.w.g.		FUSE amp.	
① 0·8	1/32	⑧ 0·25	0·010	⑭ 0·50	0·020	⑲ 22		㉓ 5	
② 1·5	1/16	⑨ 0·38	0·015	⑮ 1·00	0·040	⑳ 20		㉔ 15	
③ 2·5	3/92	⑩ 0·50	0·020	⑯ Sprue		㉑ 18		㉕ 20	
④ 3·0	1/8	⑪ 1·00	0·040	**DOWEL**		㉒ 44 Copper		㉖ 30	
⑤ 6·0	1/4	⑫ 1·50	0·060	m.m.	in.	**STEEL BOLTS**			
⑥ 9·0	3/8	⑬ 2·00	0·080	⑰ 3·0	1/8	m.m.		in.	
⑦ 25×25	1×1 sq.			⑱ 9·0	3/8	㉗ 2·5		3/32	

Finishing

Most Nieuports were clear doped all over. Later aircraft, however, had the upper surfaces of the wings painted dark green or camouflaged. French and British aircraft had roundels on top of the upper and underneath the lower wings, although British aircraft had additional roundels on the fuselage. The model is finished in the colours of the French pilot Jean Navarre, who was France's first ace.

Start by drilling the valve access holes in the wheel-covers and gluing on the control surfaces. Cut the fuel-filler cap from plastic rod and glue it to the top of the cowling. Paint the flying surfaces beige and the inside of the cockpit matt green. Apart from the cowling and top forward panel, which are silver, the rest of the fuselage is painted red. Also paint the red and blue vertical insignia stripes on the rudder. The remaining white stripe need not be painted if the rudder has been constructed from white plastic card.

Paint tan coloured the wing and undercarriage struts, tail-skid, propeller, and control horns.

Mark on the position of the white wing strut bands and paint them. The machine gun, struts, aileron control cranks and engine are painted dark grey. Paint in silver the tail-plane struts, wing strut brackets, propeller boss, engine pushrods, and the footstep surround. The cockpit padding is dark brown and tyres light grey. The wheel-covers are the same colour as the flying surfaces, with the valve holes picked out in black. The engine breather pipes and tail-skid banding are also grey.

Apply the French transfer roundels and pencil on the rib detail on top of the fuselage. Mark the stitching on the wheel-covers with a pencil and the stitching on the fuselage with black ink for contrast. Dry transfers are used for the serial number on the rudder and further details such as cowling rivets and fastenings are shown with black ink.

Semi-gloss varnish the wings and tail-plane. The fuselage is coated with matt varnish. Glue on the wheels and fasten the engine and propeller assembly inside the cowling. Cut the circular mirror from plastic rod and glue to the starboard rear centre wing strut; paint it grey and the glass silver. Measure and cut the rigging and control wires, starting at the undercarriage, centre section, wings, and finally the control wires. Use 15 amp. fuse-wire or plastic rod for the vertical aileron controls and glue them between the fuselage top and underside of the upper wings.

Paint the cockpit seat matt brown and glue in position, together with the control column and other appropriate fittings made from fuse-wire and plastic rod, suitably painted. The map table is made from plastic card, painted tan coloured, and glued under the forward edge of the cockpit. Thin paper is cut out for the map and details marked on in pencil and glued to the table; then coat them with matt varnish.

twelve
Albatros DIII

Introduction

The plywood-covered semi-monocoque fuselage, with its propeller spinner and cruciform tail surfaces, resulted in a sturdy
and streamlined aircraft. Wings were covered with fabric, as
was the tail-plane. Plywood was used for the fin and tail-skid
fairing. The undercarriage and wing struts were made of tubular
steel. A 160h.p. Mercedes six cylinder in line water-cooled
engine provided the power. On early machines the radiator was
mounted in the centre section of the upper wing. This, however, was later offset to avoid boiling water scalding the pilot if
the plumbing was shot through by stray bullets. When the
aircraft entered service in January 1917 it wrought havoc with its
twin Spandau machine guns against the comparatively lightly
armed allied reconnaissance and observation aircraft, but by the
autumn the aircraft was outclassed by the Camels, Spads and
SE5a's.

35 Albatros D111.

A combination of plastic card and balsa wood is used for modelling the Albatros, and with its deep fuselage it is possible to fit a small electric motor inside to turn the propeller, thus giving the model added realism.

Materials

Fuselage, 25 × 25mm (1 × 1in.) balsa block, and 2.5mm ($\frac{3}{32}$in.) sheet balsa.

Wing and tail-plane cores, 2.5mm ($\frac{3}{32}$in.) sheet balsa.

Fin and tail-skid fairing, 2.5mm ($\frac{3}{32}$in.) sheet balsa.

Wings and tail-plane, 0.25mm (0.010in.) plastic card.

Wheels, 1.00mm (0.040in.) and 0.50mm (0.020in.) plastic card.

Wheel-covers, 0.25mm (0.010in.) moulded plastic card.

Wing and undercarriage struts, 0.50mm (0.020in.) and 1.00mm (0.040in.) plastic rod.

Motor hatch, 0.50mm (0.020in.) plastic card.

Seat, 1.00mm (0.040in.) and 0.25mm (0.010in.) plastic card.

Propeller, 0.8mm ($\frac{1}{32}$in.) sheet balsa (laminated).

Propeller shaft, brass tube to fit over electric motor axle.

Small 1.5V. electric motor.

Engine cylinders, 3.0mm ($\frac{1}{8}$in.) birch dowel.

Exhausts, control and rigging wires, stretched plastic sprue.

Windscreen, clear acetate sheet.

36 Carved fuselage and electric motor assembly.

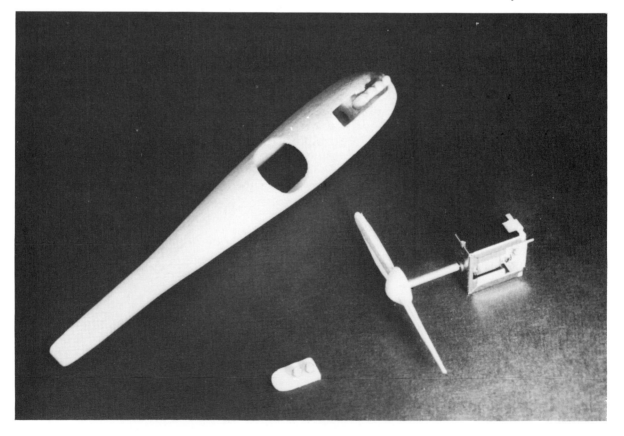

Construction

To simplify the construction of the double curvature fuselage, carve the block balsa down to the correct shape. Cut a suitable length of 25 × 25mm (1 × 1in.) block balsa, and glue a layer of 2.5mm ($\frac{3}{32}$in.) sheet balsa along the bottom to the same length and width. This will give adequate depth to the fuselage.

Trace the outline of the fuselage onto one side of the block, including the spinner, and cut it out ensuring that all faces are at right angles. Mark along the top of the block a centre line and trace on the fuselage width, again including the spinner, and cut out.

Shape and round the contours, checking against the cross-sections shown on the plan, and smooth down.

Drill and carve out the cockpit, including the engine bay and the space for the electric motor in the bottom of the fuselage. Cut off the spinner and laminate alternating layers of stained and unstained 0.8mm ($\frac{1}{32}$in.) sheet balsa together to form the propeller, and cut out and shape. Glue into slots cut in each side of the spinner.

Drill an over-sized hole centrally through the front of the fuselage for the propeller shaft to pass through. Epoxy the brass tube shaft into the back of the spinner, making sure that it is central and straight. Insert the electric motor through the hollowed out hatch in the bottom of the fuselage and align the motor so that the axle protrudes forward into the propeller shaft hole. Cut the propeller shaft to the correct length so that it will fit snuggly over the motor axle. Before fitting the motor permanently in the fuselage, solder wire leads to the motor terminals. Contact glue is suitable for fastening the motor. The balsa, however, should be sealed first with a layer of balsa cement to ensure a good bond. Finally, apply a drop of contact glue into the propeller shaft and push it into position over the motor axle. Check that the propeller rotates freely. Cut the wire leads to a suitable length and pass them through pre-drilled holes at the rear of the motor hatch and epoxy in place. When set, trim down the wires so they protrude about 2.0mm. These will provide the terminals for wiring up to a battery when the model is completed.

Cut the six engine cylinders to length from 3.0mm ($\frac{1}{8}$in.) birch dowel and glue to the base of the engine bay. The rear cylinders will probably need to be cut shorter owing to the electric motor being in the way. These cylinders are glued onto a piece of thin sheet balsa to hide the motor. Cut the motor hatch from 0.50mm (0.020in.) plastic card so that it is a spring fit and is flush with the fuselage.

Trace and cut out the forward part of the fin and the tail-skid fairing from 2.5mm ($\frac{3}{32}$in.) sheet balsa and glue to the fuselage after first shaping it to an aerofoil section. The tail-skid itself is constructed from 1.00mm (0.040in.) plastic rod and glued to the fairing.

Mark the positions of the centre wing section struts and undercarriage struts on the fuselage. Cut short lengths of 1.00mm (0.040in.) plastic rod and glue into pre-drilled holes in

Albatros D.III.

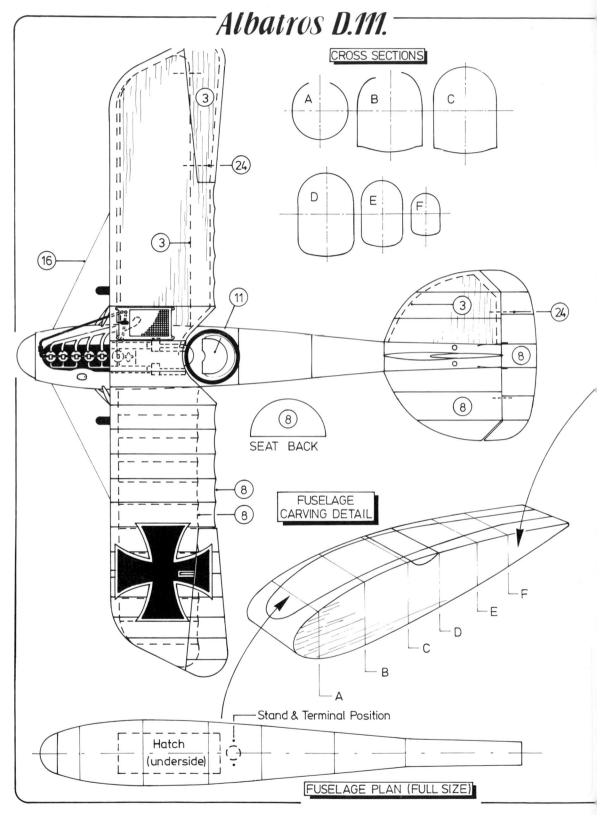

CROSS SECTIONS

A   B   C

D   E   F

SEAT BACK

FUSELAGE
CARVING DETAIL

F
E
D
C
B
A

— Stand & Terminal Position

Hatch
(underside)

FUSELAGE PLAN (FULL SIZE)

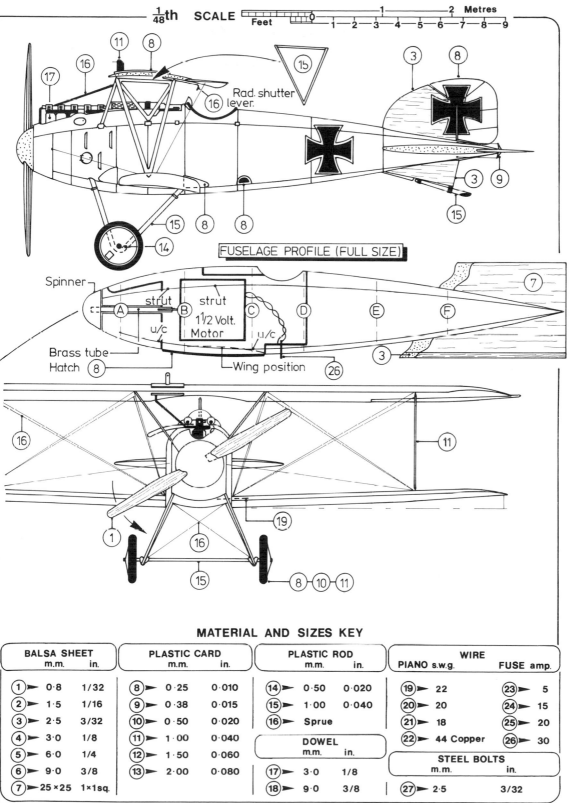

$\frac{1}{48}$th SCALE

Feet — Metres

Rad. shutter lever.

FUSELAGE PROFILE (FULL SIZE)

Spinner

strut
strut
1½ Volt.
Motor

u/c
u/c

Brass tube
Hatch ⑧

Wing position

MATERIAL AND SIZES KEY

BALSA SHEET		PLASTIC CARD		PLASTIC ROD		WIRE			
m.m.	in.	m.m.	in.	m.m.	in.	PIANO s.w.g.		FUSE amp.	
① 0·8	1/32	⑧ 0·25	0·010	⑭ 0·50	0·020	⑲ 22		㉓ 5	
② 1·5	1/16	⑨ 0·38	0·015	⑮ 1·00	0·040	⑳ 20		㉔ 15	
③ 2·5	3/32	⑩ 0·50	0·020	⑯ Sprue		㉑ 18		㉕ 20	
④ 3·0	1/8	⑪ 1·00	0·040	**DOWEL**		㉒ 44 Copper		㉖ 30	
⑤ 6·0	1/4	⑫ 1·50	0·060	m.m.	in.	**STEEL BOLTS**			
⑥ 9·0	3/8	⑬ 2·00	0·080	⑰ 3·0	1/8	m.m.		in.	
⑦ 25×25	1×1sq.			⑱ 9·0	3/8	㉗ 2·5		3/32	

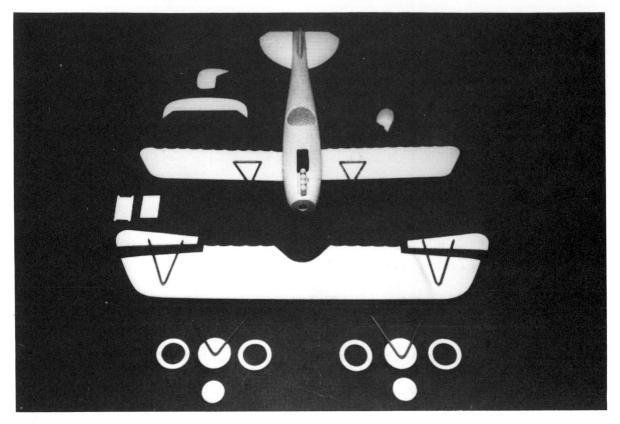

37 Parts ready for painting and assembly.

the marked positions. These will provide anchor points for gluing the struts too.

All the struts are constructed from 1.00mm (0.040in.) plastic rod, except for the undercarriage axle support which is 0.50mm (0.020in.) plastic rod. Cut and bend the two undercarriage vee struts over the plan and glue to each side of the fuselage. Cut to length the axle and support, and glue between the two vee struts.

Construct the two triangular centre wing section struts over the plan, together with the two outboard vee wing struts. When bending sharp corners in the struts, dab the plastic rod against a hot electric light bulb. This will enable the bend to be made exactly in the right spot.

The wings and tail-plane are constructed from 0.25mm (0.010in.) plastic card over 2.5mm ($\frac{3}{32}$in.) sheet balsa cores, using the method described in the chapter on techniques. Mark the positions of the lower wings on the fuselage sides and cut two short lengths of 22g. piano-wire lugs pushed into each wing root. Push the protruding wing lugs into the fuselage sides and glue them to the dihedral shown on the plan. Mark and drill the positions of the outer wing struts between each wing. Cut out the two ailerons on the top wing and glue the triangular centre section struts to the underside to angle shown on the plan, at the same time checking they meet at their attachment points on the fuselage. Locate the upper wing, temporarily supported with Blu-Tack on the fuselage, and glue the outer struts in place, as well as the two single forward centre section struts cut from plastic rod.

Trace and cut out the two halves of the elevator and score the insides of the plastic card for the ribbing effect and glue together. Cut the control horns from 0.38mm (0.015in.) plastic card and glue to both upper and lower surfaces. Repeat for the rudder, except make a third layer: this middle layer is shaped to an aerofoil section with the outer ribbed layers glued to each side. Glue the tail-plane to each side of the fuselage and trim the trailing edge if necessary for the elevator to fit. The tail-plane is glued in position, together with the ailerons after the painting is finished.

Some details can be made at this stage and fitted, such as the radiator, which is constructed from 0.25mm (0.010in.) plastic card and glued to both surfaces of the upper wing, offset as shown. The seat is also made from plastic card as specified on the plan. The wheel-covers are moulded by heating 0.25mm (0.010in.) plastic card over a circle cut in scrap sheet balsa and plunging a shaped male mould into it. Cut the wheels from 1.00mm (0.040in.) and tyres from 0.50mm (0.020in.) plastic card, glued together and shaped.

38 Motor installation (note connecting terminals).

Finishing

The standard factory finish was varnished plywood fuselage and fin, with grey or olive green cowling and metal fittings. Upper flying surfaces were usually dark green with mauve patches. Undersurfaces were pale blue. As with quite a few German aircraft of the period, pilots applied their own distinctive colour schemes. The model described here represents a variation on the standard finish and shows off the varnished plywood fuselage with contrasting polished alloy cowling and black tail-plane.

Stain the fuselage with mahogany coloured dye, apply two coats of sanding sealer and smooth down with fine glasspaper. Also apply two coats to the propeller and smooth down. Do not stain the propeller, otherwise the contrasting laminated veneers will not stand out. Apply one or two coats of clear varnish as required to the fuselage.

Attach the control surfaces to the upper wings and tail-plane with fuse-wire and position to the desired angle. If necessary apply a drop of glue to prevent movement. Cut out the elevator control horns from scrap plastic card and glue in position.

Paint the undersides of the wings light blue and the topsides dark green with mauve patches. The struts and undercarriage, including the wheels, are also dark green. Mark on the boundary lines of the black tail-plane, nose band, and the alloy cowling and paint. Apply alloy paint to the radiator and propeller spinner, and mark on the fuselage panel lines with a ruling pen and black ink. Cut a small straight edge from scrap plastic card to aid marking. The circular inspection hatches are marked on with the aid of a stencil, also cut from plastic card. Paint the tyres and tail-skid tip grey. The tail-skid itself is tan coloured, as is the cockpit padding, which is made from rolled out modelling filler and glued in place.

Apply the cross insignia transfers and coat the wings, struts, and undercarriage, including the wheels and tail-skid with matt varnish. Coat the fuselage and tail-plane with semi-matt varnish, and the alloy cowling, propeller and spinner with gloss varnish.

Cut and bend the exhaust pipe and stubs from plastic rod and sprue; paint this and the radiator piping, made from 30 amp. fuse-wire, copper colour. Paint the inside of the engine well matt black. The cylinders are dark brown with the valves, made from plastic sprue, picked out in dull silver and black. The inlet manifolds are a dull copper colour. Position the exhaust and radiator piping with glue and also the machine-guns, constructed from plastic rod and card and painted dark grey.

Cut out the windscreen from clear acetate sheet and glue it directly in front of the cockpit. Measure and cut to length the control and rigging wires from stretched plastic sprue and glue them in position as shown, starting at the undercarriage and centre section. Add the cockpit details, constructed from plastic rod and card, suitably painted. Paint the pilot seat dark matt green and glue it against the rear of the cockpit opening. The pilot is a white metal figure obtained commercially and painted.

Finally, cut out the footstep (port side only) and wing root plates from thin plastic card, painted matt grey and glued in position.

Construct the display stand as described in the chapter on displaying models. Certain modifications, however, are needed to house the battery to power the motor. These include the cut out section in the base where the battery is located and the partition part 'B'. Brass or copper strip is used for the battery contacts; these are glued one each side of the partition as shown with the switch bolted through the top. The brass tube support also carries the wires from the base to the motor, so it may be necessary to fasten a larger diameter tube in the base than normal. Drill two holes in the clevis and thread two thin connecting-wires through the tube and out through the clevis. Glue the clevis to the tube and glue the bottom of the tube through a pre-drilled hole in the base and balsa packing. Solder the wires in series to the switch and battery contacts. Clip the model on to the clevis and solder the protruding wires to the two terminals on the underside of the fuselage. Leave sufficient lengths of wire to allow the model to be positioned at various angles. As a final touch, cut a thin strip of tissue paper for a scarf and lightly glue it to the pilot, leaving about 2cm flaying out. The scarf will then realistically wave in the slipstream when the motor is switched on.

39 Starboard side showing engine exhaust.

thirteen
Fokker Dr 1 Triplane

Introduction

The triple wing design first appeared in the War in the shape of the Sopwith Triplane. This arrangement gave the aircraft superior climbing ability as well as excellent lateral manoeuvrability afforded by the reduced wingspan. Such was the success of the Sopwith Triplane, the German authorities wanted a comparable aircraft. Anthony Fokker answered the need with his Dr 1 Dreidecker design, which, unlike the Sopwith, dispensed with the normal drag-producing rigging wires. This was achieved by constructing the cantilevered wings around deep-section hollow box spars, and without interplane struts. Although this arrangement proved to be very robust, interplane struts were re-introduced to prevent vibration and improve control.

By the end of August 1917 deliveries of the aircraft had begun. Its superior agility appealed to the experienced pilots, although it was slower than its contemporaries and was outclassed by May 1918 when production ended.

40 Fokker Triplane.

The Fokker DV III is a suitable model for beginners to build. Balsa wood is used for its construction, and transfers provide the lozenge camouflage effect.

1/48th scale Fokker Dr I triplane shown against 7.92mm Spandau machine-gun bullets used on the full sized aircraft.

Felixstowe F2A flying boat constructed from balsa wood and plastic card to 1/72nd scale and rigged with 44 gauge copper wire.

Stained strip balsa wood is used for the Blériot XI fuselage with plastic card panels and wings.

The powerplant was usually a 110 h.p. nine cylinder rotary Le Rhône engine, which gave a top speed of 165 kmh (103.12 mph). Armament consisted of two Spandau 7.92mm machine guns mounted on the fuselage.

Modelling the Dr 1 in plastic card is fairly straightforward. The fuselage is built up from a basic box and the cowling and curved side panels added. Sheet balsa is used for the wing cores and propeller. The engine and machine guns are white metal fittings obtained commercially.

Materials

Fuselage, pilot seat, 0.50mm (0.020in.), and 0.25mm (0.010in.) plastic card.

Cowling, 1.00mm (0.040in.), and 0.25mm (0.010in.) plastic card.

Wings, tail-plane, rudder, axle fairing, 0.25mm (0.010in.) plastic card.

Wing struts, tail-plane packing, control horns, 0.38mm (0.015in.) plastic card.

Undercarriage and centre section struts, tail-skid, axle, 1.00mm (0.040in.) plastic rod.

Tail-plane bracing, wing skids, 0.50mm (0.020in.) plastic rod.

Wing cores, 2.5mm ($\frac{3}{32}$in.) sheet balsa.

Wing lugs, 22 gauge piano-wire.

Wheels, 1.00mm (0.040in.), and 0.50mm (0.020in.) plastic card.

Wheel covers, 0.38mm (0.015in.) moulded plastic card.

Propeller, 3.0mm ($\frac{1}{8}$in.) sheet balsa.

Control wires etc. stretched plastic sprue.

Construction

Trace and cut out the fuselage sides, bottom, and frames, (A), (B), and (C), from plastic card as specified. Mark on the fuselage sides the positions of frames (B) and (C), and glue them together with frame (A) and the rear pointed end of the fuselage. Hold them together with tape until set. Trace and cut out the bottom and glue in position. Trim off any excess if necessary when set.

Cut out the two cowling cheek formers from 0.50mm (0.020in.) plastic card and glue them to each side of frame (A). Cut out the front top deck and sides from paper. Trim to fit round the fuselage. The front of the fuselage should be round in section, tapering to a flat section against the fuselage sides at the cockpit. When correctly fitted, use the paper as a template for cutting out the part from 0.25mm (0.010in.) plastic card. Fasten it in place by first gluing it centrally on top of the fuselage and, holding it down with tape, glue down the sides.

Similarly cut out the rear top deck from the same thickness plastic card and glue it in place, butting up against the front deck. It may be helpful first to cut out a support from plastic card the same shape as the top of frame (B) that is glued against that frame to provide a ledge for gluing the deck to. When set, mark and cut out the cockpit. Cut out a plastic card support, the

Fokker Dr 1. Triplane

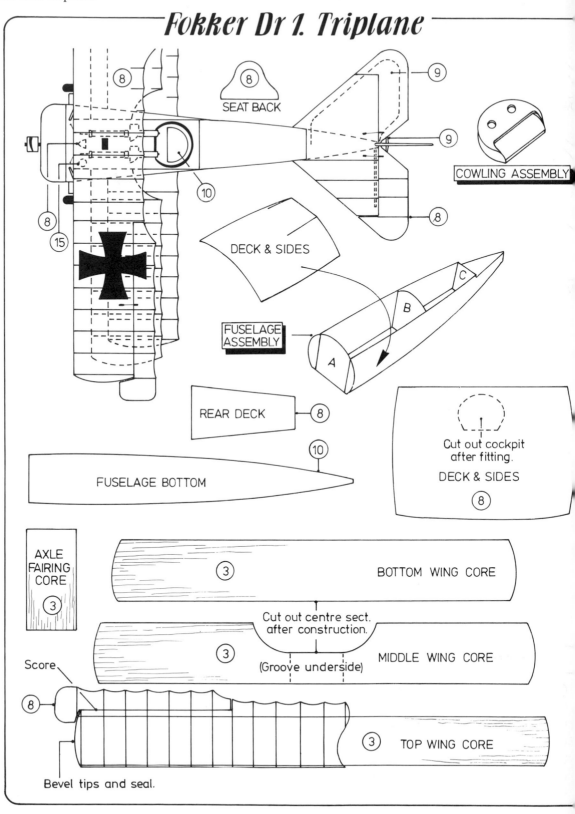

8

8
SEAT BACK

9

9

COWLING ASSEMBLY

10

8

8

15

DECK & SIDES

FUSELAGE
ASSEMBLY

A

B

C

REAR DECK   8

10

Cut out cockpit
after fitting.
DECK & SIDES
8

FUSELAGE BOTTOM

AXLE
FAIRING
CORE
3

BOTTOM WING CORE
3

Cut out centre sect.
after construction.
3
(Groove underside)   MIDDLE WING CORE

Score

8

Bevel tips and seal.

3   TOP WING CORE

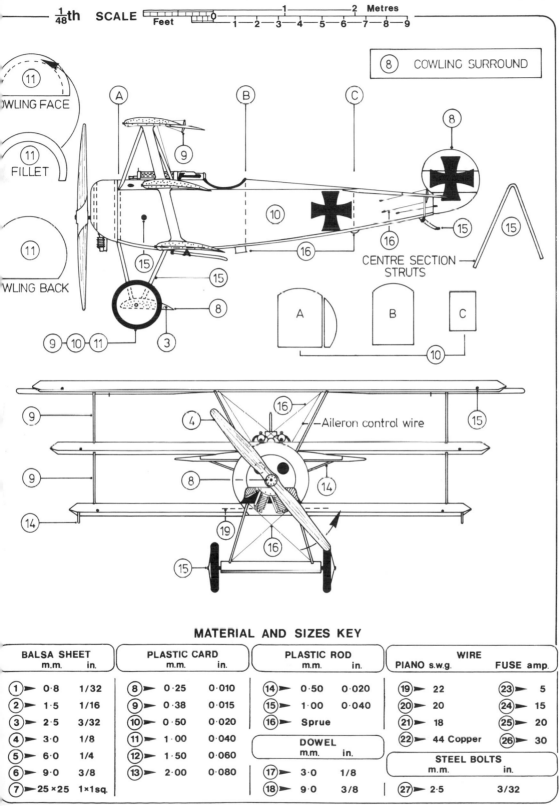

$\frac{1}{48}$th SCALE

8 COWLING SURROUND

COWLING FACE

FILLET

COWLING BACK

CENTRE SECTION STRUTS

Aileron control wire

MATERIAL AND SIZES KEY

BALSA SHEET			PLASTIC CARD			PLASTIC ROD			WIRE			
	m.m.	in.		m.m.	in.		m.m.	in.	PIANO s.w.g.		FUSE amp.	
1	0·8	1/32	8	0·25	0·010	14	0·50	0·020	19	22	23	5
2	1·5	1/16	9	0·38	0·015	15	1·00	0·040	20	20	24	15
3	2·5	3/32	10	0·50	0·020	16	Sprue		21	18	25	20
4	3·0	1/8	11	1·00	0·040	DOWEL			22	44 Copper	26	30
5	6·0	1/4	12	1·50	0·060		m.m.	in.	STEEL BOLTS			
6	9·0	3/8	13	2·00	0·080	17	3·0	1/8		m.m.		in.
7	25×25	1×1sq.				18	9·0	3/8	27	2·5		3/92

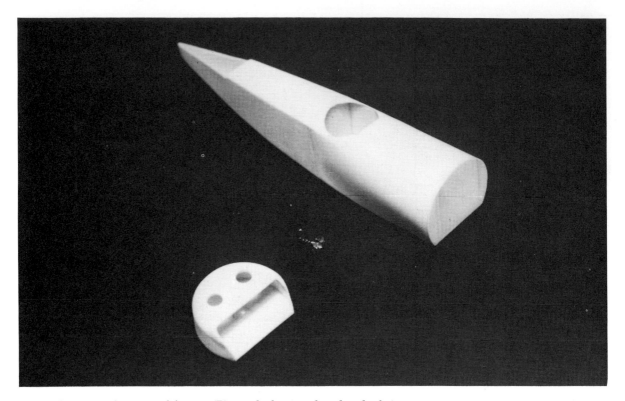

same shape as the top of frame (B), and glue under the deck in front of the cockpit.

Trace and cut out the cowling back from 1.00mm (0.040in.) plastic card, together with two laminations of the cowling front from the same thickness of plastic card. The inner lamination is crescent shaped and is glued to the rear of the cowling face. Mark out the cowling sides from 0.25mm (0.010in.) plastic card, and glue round the back. When set, glue the face in position and shape the lower edges of the sides. Glue the completed cowling to the front of the fuselage, fair in sides and round off the face.

Finish the fuselage by fairing in the curved side panels where they meet the flat side sections of the fuselage at the cockpit and smooth all corners.

Trace and cut out from 0.25mm (0.010in.) plastic card both halves of the tail-plane and rudder. Score the rib detail on the inside of each half and glue together with a piece of 0.38mm (0.015in.) plastic card between the tail-plane halves only to give the correct thickness. Score and cut the elevator and set it to the desired angle. Smooth off edges and glue in place.

Mark out the three wings, including the axle fairing on 0.25mm (0.010in.) plastic card. Cut out and score rib detail and attach with double sided tape around the 2.5mm ($\frac{3}{32}$in.) balsa cores. The wings are in three continuous lengths, except for the centre section of the lower wing, which is cut away after constructing the wings. Only the trailing edges are glued together, the tips are bevelled as shown and the exposed balsa cores sealed with polystyrene cement. Cut out a groove in the under-

41 Fuselage and cowling assembly.

side of the middle wing to make it sit centrally on top of the
fuselage. Seal the exposed balsa core with polystyrene cement.
Score and cut the ailerons in the top wing and set them to the
desired angle.

Mark on the fuselage the positions of the lower and middle
wings. Cut a suitable length of 22g. piano-wire for the lower
wing lugs and glue them into the fuselage through pre-drilled
holes. Shape the lower wing roots, push them over the lugs and
glue them to the fuselage sides. Glue the middle wing on top of
the fuselage, checking that it is square with the lower wings.

Cut and bend the two inverted centre section vee struts from
1.00mm (0.040in.) plastic rod and file to an oval section. Mark
their positions on top of the fuselage and glue into pre-drilled
holes at the angle shown. Cut out the four interplane struts from
0.38mm (0.015in.) plastic card and glue them between the lower
and middle wings where shown. Glue the remaining two struts
on top of the middle wing, in line with the lower struts. Glue the
upper wing on top of the interplane and centre section struts,
checking that it is square with the remaining wings.

Mark on the fuselage and the axle fairing the position of the
undercarriage struts. These are cut from 1.00mm (0.040in.) plastic rod, sanded to an oval section and first glued into the top of
the axle fairing through pre-drilled holes at the correct angle.
When set, locate and glue the top of the struts into the fuselage
through pre-drilled holes. Cut to length the two stub axles from
1.00mm (0.040in.) plastic rod and glue into a pre-drilled hole in
each end of the fairing through the balsa core.

42 Constructing and fitting
   wings.

43 Model ready for painting and detailing.

Owing to the absence of rigging wires, most of the details can now be added. These include the tail and wing-skids, tail-plane bracing, wing pads on the leading edges, which are all from plastic rod as specified. The footstep and lifting handles are made from stretched plastic sprue. Cut out the control horns from 0.38mm (0.015in.) plastic card and glue them to both sides of the ailerons, elevator, and rudder. The wheels and pilots seat are made from plastic card as specified, and the propeller carved from 3.0mm ($\frac{1}{8}$in.) sheet balsa. Blu-Tack is used for the cockpit padding and under each side of the middle wing where it meets the fuselage. Seal the padding with thinned-down polystyrene cement.

Finishing

Cut out the fuel gauge fairing and propeller boss from thin plastic card and also the fuel filler cap from plastic rod. Plastic tubing is used for the engine breather pipe and all these items, with the exception of the propeller boss, are glued in place.

The standard colour scheme for these aircraft seemed to be light blue under surfaces, with the upper surfaces and sides of the fuselage in streaky dark green camouflage painted over natural doped fabric (beige). A few of the more flamboyant pilots, however, had their aircraft painted in bright colours, which arguably made them more attractive. The famous ace Manfred von Richofen, who was killed in action in late April 1918, piloted an all red aircraft (dubbed "The Red Baron" by the allied pilots) which the below model represents.

Apply at least two coats of red enamel to the entire model and apply the cross insignia transfers etc. Mark in pencil the control hinge lines, spoke and stitching detail to the underside of the fuselage. Lightly shade in soft pencil the weathering, dirt and oil marks by the cockpit and cowling areas and smudge to give the required effect. Coat the model with clear matt varnish, except for the cowling and propeller, which are varnished with gloss. The propeller is stained with mahogany dye before it is varnished.

Measure and cut to length from stretched plastic spruc the control and rigging wires and glue where shown. These are painted with thinned brown enamel.

Paint the following items: the cockpit padding, seat, tail and wing skids—matt brown; the engine bay, cylinders, handles, and footstep—matt black; the tyres, tail-skid tip, control horns, machine guns—matt grey; the engine crank case and propeller boss—silver; and the exhaust pipes—burnt copper.

Fasten the engine in the cowling with a short piece of brass tube over the propeller shaft, glued into a pre-cut notch in the cowling. Glue the propeller and boss to the end of the protruding shaft. The engine and propeller should rotate freely in the brass tube. Apply a drop of oil to the shaft if necessary.

Glue the machine guns to the fuselage, decking together with the windscreen cut from clear acetate sheet. Glue the wheels on the axles and add cockpit detail, which includes the seat, control column, throttle lever, instrumentation, and compass, all made from scrap plastic card and suitably painted before fitting.

44 Rear view showing general dirt and oil stain effects on the fuselage.

fourteen
Blériot X1

Introduction

Louis Blériot is probably remembered for his famous crossing of the English Channel in 1909. The aircraft in a modified form contributed to the formation of Britain's first air force in February 1911. In the company of six Boxkites, a Henri Farman and an old reconstructed Howard Wright biplane, volunteer pilots had to learn to fly these aircraft at their own expense. If they were successful the government repaid the costs.

By order of things, this project should really have appeared at the beginning of the book. From a modelling viewpoint, however, this and other very early types are a little more tricky to build owing to the *uncovered* nature of the fuselage. The structure and internal wire bracing, therefore, must be reproduced as well as spoked wheels and a sometimes complicated undercarriage structure.

Although building the Blériot requires a certain amount of dexterity, the model should not present many problems. The fuselage is a simple box structure based on four balsa longitudinal members running the length of the fuselage. Wings, tailplane and rudder are made from plastic card, and the undercarriage structure is produced from plastic rod.

45 Blériot XI.

Materials

Fuselage, 0.8mm ($\frac{1}{32}$in.) sq balsa strip, and 0.25mm (0.010in.)
   plastic card.
Wings, tail-plane and rudder, 1.00mm (0.040in.) and
   0.25mm (0.010in.) plastic card.
Undercarriage, pylon and tail-skid, 1.00mm (0.040in.) plastic
   card and rod, and 0.50mm (0.020in.) plastic rod.
Wheels, 0.50mm (0.020in.) plastic card and clear acetate sheet.
Wheel spokes, 5 amp. fuse-wire.
Wheel hubs, 0.25mm (0.010in.) plastic card.
Engine block and bracket, 1.00mm (0.040in.) plastic card
   (laminated).
Cylinders, three 2.5mm ($\frac{3}{32}$in.) cut down bolts.
Pushrods and exhausts, 15 amp. fuse-wire.
Fuel tank, 6.0mm ($\frac{1}{4}$in.) balsa dowel.
Propeller, 3.0mm ($\frac{1}{8}$in.) sheet balsa.
Pilot seat and control horns, 0.50mm (0.020in.),
   0.38mm (0.015in.), and 0.25mm (0.010in.) plastic card.
Control and rigging wires, 5 amp. fuse-wire.

Construction

The fuselage framework is constructed from 0.8mm ($\frac{1}{32}$in.) sq.
balsa strip. This can be obtained ready cut or made by cutting
parallel strips from sheet balsa of the same thickness. Cover the
plan with clear film or tracing paper, as the two fuselage sides
are constructed over the plan and the film will prevent the parts
sticking to the plan itself. Cut to length both the upper and
lower longitudinal members and tape over the plan.
   Cut from 0.8mm ($\frac{1}{32}$in.) sq. balsa strip the nine vertical bracing
members, which include the tail-post and longer undercarriage

46 Constructing fuselage sides
   over the plan.

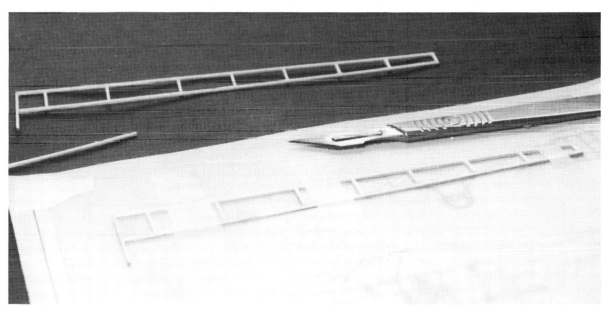

Bleriot X1

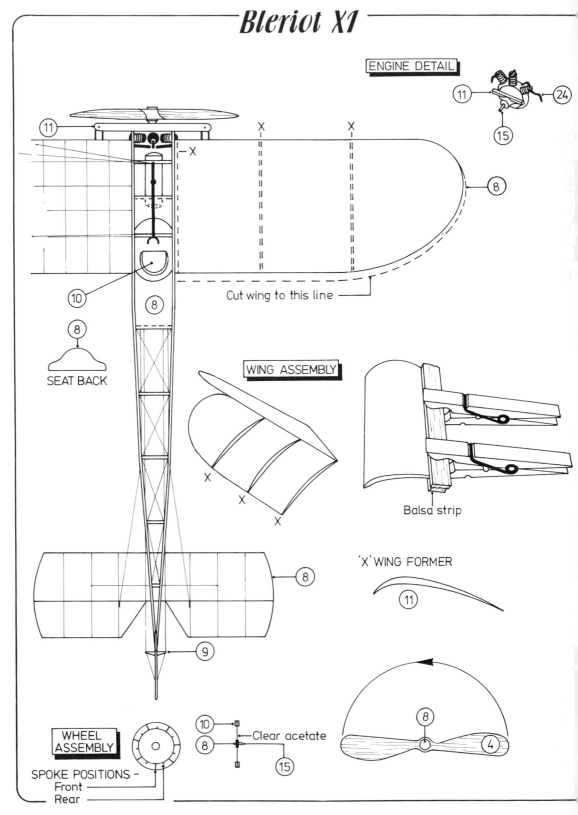

ENGINE DETAIL

Cut wing to this line

SEAT BACK

WING ASSEMBLY

Balsa strip

'X' WING FORMER

WHEEL ASSEMBLY

SPOKE POSITIONS –
Front
Rear

Clear acetate

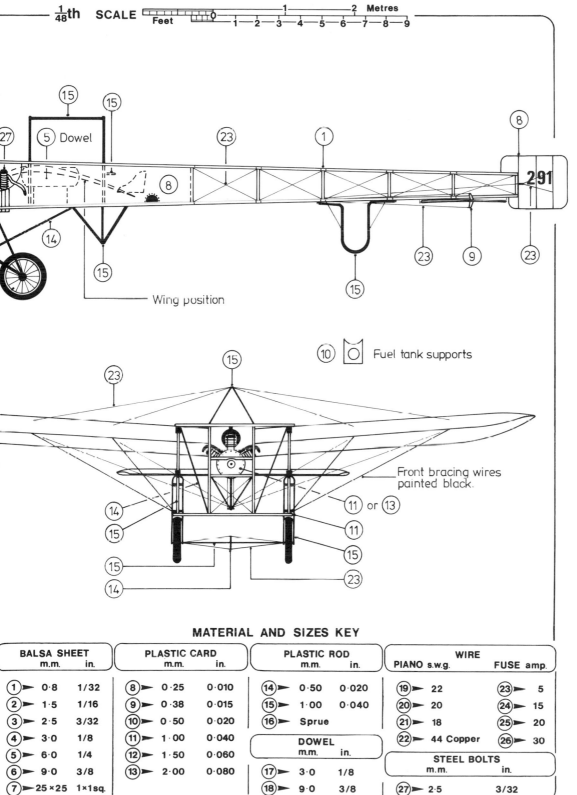

$\frac{1}{48}$th **SCALE**

Feet

Metres

⑮ ⑮

㉗ ⑤ Dowel

㉓ ① ⑧

291

⑧

⑭

⑮ Wing position

⑩ Fuel tank supports

㉓ ⑮

Front bracing wires painted black.

⑭

⑮ ⑪ or ⑬

⑪

⑮ ⑮

⑮ ㉓

⑭

MATERIAL AND SIZES KEY

BALSA SHEET		PLASTIC CARD		PLASTIC ROD		WIRE			
m.m.	in.	m.m.	in.	m.m.	in.	PIANO s.w.g.		FUSE amp.	
①▶ 0·8	1/32	⑧▶ 0·25	0·010	⑭▶ 0·50	0·020	⑲▶ 22		㉓▶ 5	
②▶ 1·5	1/16	⑨▶ 0·38	0·015	⑮▶ 1·00	0·040	⑳▶ 20		㉔▶ 15	
③▶ 2·5	3/32	⑩▶ 0·50	0·020	⑯▶ Sprue		㉑▶ 18		㉕▶ 20	
④▶ 3·0	1/8	⑪▶ 1·00	0·040	**DOWEL**		㉒▶ 44 Copper		㉖▶ 30	
⑤▶ 6·0	1/4	⑫▶ 1·50	0·060	m.m.	in.	**STEEL BOLTS**			
⑥▶ 9·0	3/8	⑬▶ 2·00	0·080	⑰▶ 3·0	1/8	m.m.		in.	
⑦▶ 25×25	1×1sq.			⑱▶ 9·0	3/8	㉗▶ 2·5		3/32	

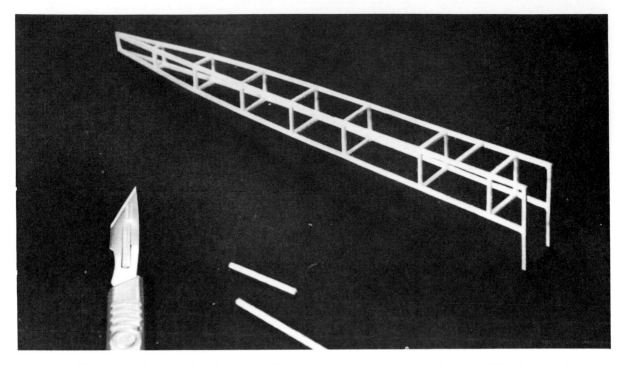

support. Glue these in position between the upper and lower longitudinal members over the plan; P.V.A. glue is best for this. When set, remove the side of the fuselage from the plan using a knife. Sand down the joints on both sides and remove any excess glue. Repeat the procedure for the other fuselage side.

Bevel the inside edges of the tail-posts on each side of the fuselage and glue them together over the plan. Cut to length the seven top and seven bottom cross-members from 0.8mm ($\frac{1}{32}$in.) sq. balsa strip. Glue in position, starting from the front and working back to the rear, ensuring that the sides of the fuselage remain level and the cross-members square. Finally, cut out and glue the cockpit cross-member in position on top of the fuselage. Sand down the joints and entire frame and stain the balsa with mahogany wood dye.

Trace and cut out from 0.25mm (0.010in.) plastic card the forward covered sections of the fuselage sides, bottom and top, including the cockpit opening, and glue to the fuselage frame. Cut and bend to shape the tail-skid from 1.00mm (0.040in.) plastic rod and glue to the bottom cross-members where shown. (When gluing plastic to wood, coat the wood first with a layer of polystyrene cement and use solvent to fasten the plastic in the required position.)

Cut and bend the top and bottom pylon vee struts from 1.00mm (0.040in.) plastic rod and glue in the positions shown. Link the two top inverted vee struts together with the same thickness of plastic rod. Cut the control column to length from plastic rod, as well as the handle, and glue them through a pre-drilled hole in the bottom of the fuselage into the apex of the lower pylon.

47 Completed fuselage ready for covering the cockpit area.

Trace and cut out the wings from 0.25mm (0.010in.) plastic card. Cut the underside of the wings to the exact size shown on the plan. The top surface is cut slightly oversize to allow for curvature and is trimmed after gluing together. Fold the wings along their leading edges and mark on the lower surfaces the positions of wing ribs (three to each wing). Trace and cut out the wing ribs from 1.00mm (0.040in.) plastic card and first glue them to the lower wing surfaces, and then glue and fold over the upper surfaces. When set, trim and smooth edges by sanding. Slightly bevel each wing root to give the required dihedral and glue the wings to the fuselage sides where shown.

Trace and cut out the two halves of the tail-plane and rudder from 0.25mm (0.010in.) plastic card. Score on the inside halves the rib detail and glue together. Round and smooth down edges and score and bend the elevator to the desired angle. Glue the tail-plane to the underside of the fuselage where shown; trim the rudder to fit against the tail-post and glue it in position.

Cut to length from 1.00mm (0.040in.) plastic card two strips of 1.50mm (0.060in.) wide main, cross-bar members for the under-carriage frame; smooth the edges round. Glue the members centrally across the front of the fuselage. The lower cross-member should have a hole drilled in each end to accept the two vertical wheel supports, cut from 1.00mm (0.040in.) plastic rod, before it is glued in place. Insert a short length of plastic lighting flex sleeving over the top ends of the wheel supports and glue it into position through the holes in the bottom member to the top member. Insert a further short length of lighting flex sleeving over the lower protruding ends of the wheel supports (these represent collars for attachment points). To complete the under-carriage frame cut the diagonal bracing from 0.50mm (0.020in.) plastic rod and glue it in the frame and between the frame and fuselage.

Cut and bend the four wheel forks from 1.00mm (0.040in.) plastic rod and glue them to the wheel supports where shown. Also glue together the bottom ends of the forks where they meet. Check that the forks are wide enough to accept the wheels and glue two spacers, cut from plastic rod, in between each of the main forks where shown. Slip over a further short piece of lighting flex sleeve where the main forks join the wheel supports (slit the sleeve down the side to get it on). Glue a short length of plastic rod to the top of each main fork for attachment of the suspension rubber. Cut the axle from 1.00mm (0.040in.) plastic rod and glue between the inside of the forks.

Most early aircraft had spoked wheels; these were usually covered in to prevent mud clogging the spokes. Obviously, it is unnecessary to show the spokes on these aircraft. Wheel covers, however, were not in use on the very early aircraft, such as the Blériot, so it is therefore necessary to show the spokes.

One of the easiest ways I have found to produce spoked wheels is to construct the wheel on a clear acetate sheet disc, the same diameter as the wheel. The tyre, made from plastic card rings, is glued to each side of the acetate disc and shaped. Small plastic card circles are cut out for the hub and glued centrally on

each side of the disc. Mark the positions of the spokes on the inside of the tyres and prick them with a pin or sharp pointed knife. In the case of the Blériot, seven spokes on each side of the wheel are cut from 5 amp. fuse-wire; one end is inserted in the tyre rim and the other end glued with P.V.A. glue to the hub. Repeat this process on both sides of the wheel until completed. Finally, glue a short length of plastic rod to the rim for the tyre valve.

Construct the engine crank case from plastic card discs laminated together and shaped. Cut three 2.5mm ($\frac{3}{32}$in.) steel bolts to length for the cylinders and screw into pre-drilled holes in the top of the crank case. Use 15 amp. fuse-wire for making the push rods, which are held in place with super glue. The engine mounting bracket is made from 1.00mm (0.040in.) plastic card, bent and shaped to fit between the two front vertical fuselage members. Glue the bracket to the top of the crank case.

Trace and cut out the propeller from 3.0mm ($\frac{1}{8}$in.) sheet balsa, and shape. Construct the propeller shaft from plastic rod and glue into a pre-drilled hole in the end of the engine crank case. The fuel tank is made from 6.0mm ($\frac{1}{4}$in.) balsa dowel and coated with balsa cement to seal the grain ready for painting. Cut out plastic card supports and glue them to the underside of the tank for mounting in the fuselage.

Construct the pilot seat from plastic card as specified, and also the six control horns which are glued to both surfaces of the elevator and rudder. No control horns are required for the wings as they are warped via wires running over the pylons.

48 Underside view showing wings and undercarriage frame fitted, with wheels under construction.

Finishing

The military version of the Blériot differed slightly from the aircraft that first crossed the English Channel. Notable differences include a larger rudder and a tail-skid rather than a wheel. A cowling partially enclosed the engine on the military versions; this has been excluded on the model, however, to show the detail of the three cylinder 35 h.p. Anzani motor that was used on the earlier types. Later military aircraft were fitted with the 60 h.p. Gnome or Le Rhône rotary engines.

Finish was natural fabric colour doped over, represented on the model by painting the wings, tail-plane, and covered section of the fuselage in beige. Paint tan the two main cross-members of the undercarriage frame and the control horns on the tail-plane. Paint matt black both the upper and lower pylon assemblies, tail-skid, wheel rims, hubs, axle and forks, and the diagonal undercarriage bracing. The vertical fork support bars, fork spacers, engine crankcase, and propeller boss (made from thin plastic card) are silver coloured.

Lightly pencil the rib detail on the wings and tail plane. Also pencil in the leading and trailing edges and smudge them to blend in with the rib detail. Use dry transfer figures to apply the serial number on the rudder. Coat the wings, fuselage and tail-plane with clear semi-gloss varnish. The balsa wood fuselage members will require two coats to finish. Stain the propeller

49 Top view also showing mirrored underside detail.

with mahogany dye and apply two or three coats of clear gloss varnish. Paint the tyres and control column grey and the seat matt brown.

Paint the fuel tank brass coloured and add the filler cap made from plastic rod, which is painted silver. Glue the tank in position and then the engine. Mount the seat on plastic rod to give it the right height and glue it inside the cockpit. Attach the propeller and retain it with the boss. Cut out the rudder suspension cord from plastic sprue and glue it to the two vertical fork support bars; paint it grey. Glue the wheels in between the forks. Cut the axle rigging spacers from thin plastic rod and glue them on each side of the axle centre.

All rigging and control wires are constructed from 5 amp. pre-rolled fuse-wire. Measure and cut the lengths starting with the control wires along inside the fuselage to the rudder and elevator horns. Next, glue in place the axle and undercarriage wires, then the diagonal fuselage bracing (transverse wires first) and then the wing bracing and warping wires. Finally, glue in place the tail-plane bracing and tail-skid stabilizing wires. Paint the axle rigging spacers and lower wing bracing wires black.

fifteen

Royal Aircraft Factory SE5a

Introduction

As with most aircraft of the period, the SE5a evolved with a number of modifications. The first flights were made in November 1916 using a 150 h.p. Hispano-Suiza engine. Owing to successive engine failures, however, the 200 h.p. V8 Wolseley Viper engine was introduced. This more powerful engine was capable of coping with the higher altitudes and could give the aircraft a maximum speed of 193.1kmh (120mph). Other modifications included the removal of the wing mounted gravity tank and the transparent cockpit hood that impaired the pilot's forward visibility.

Armament consisted of two forward-mounted Vickers 303in. machine-guns, one housed in the fuselage and the other on a Foster mounting on the centre wing section; these were sometimes aligned to give converging fire.

The SE5a shared a reputation of strength and performance with the Sopwith Camel by finally gaining air superiority over the British front in 1918.

50 SE5a.

The model is mostly made from plastic card with balsa wood wing cores and propeller. Birch dowel is used for constructing the engine cylinder fairings, and plastic sprue for the exhaust pipes etc.

Materials

Fuselage, 0.38mm (0.015in.), and 0.25mm (0.010in.) plastic card.
Cowling, radiator and tail skid, 1.00mm (0.040in.) plastic card.
Wing and undercarriage struts, 0.50mm (0.020in.) plastic card.
Wings, tail-plane, rudder, and axle fairing, 0.25mm (0.010in.) plastic card.
Wheels, 1.00mm (0.040in.), and 0.50mm (0.020in.) plastic card.
Wheel covers, 0.38mm (0.015in.) moulded plastic card.
Axle, and Foster gun mounting, 0.50mm (0.020in.), and 1.00mm (0.040in.) plastic rod.
Engine cylinder fairings, 3.0mm ($\frac{1}{8}$in.) birch dowel.
Propeller, 3.0mm ($\frac{1}{8}$in.) sheet balsa.
Exhaust pipes, control and rigging wires, stretched plastic sprue.
Windscreen, clear acetate sheet.
Wing cores, 2.5mm ($\frac{3}{32}$in.) balsa sheet.

Construction

The fuselage is basically boxed-shaped with the exception of the curved top, which is formed in two separate front and rear sections. Trace and cut out from 0.38mm (0.015in.) plastic card the fuselage sides, bottom, and frames, (A), (B), (C), and (D). Glue the frames to the sides of the fuselage in the positions shown, ensuring that they are level and square. Score and slightly bend the bottom where shown and also the sides of the fuselage at frame position (C). Glue the bottom to the underside of the fuselage and trim if necessary when set.

Cut out the two curved top sections of the fuselage from

51 Covered fuselage with cockpit marked on.

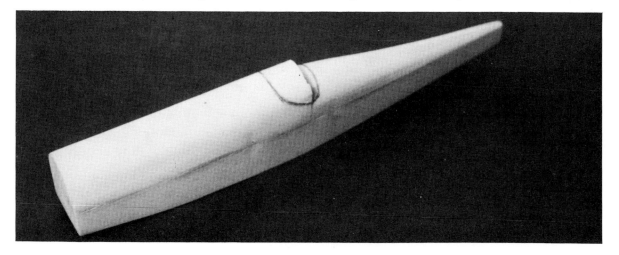

paper and trim to fit over the frames. Use the paper as a template to mark round and cut out the sections from 0.38mm (0.015in.) plastic card. Score the card to help bending and glue strips of 3mm wide card to the edges of the top sections where shown. When set the sections should clip into the fuselage sides for gluing. If necessary hold the sections in place with tape while gluing them to the frames and sides. The front and rear sections are butt-jointed together just forward of frame (C). Mark and cut out the cockpit, smooth down and fair in edges of all seams.

Trace and cut out from 1.00mm (0.040in.) plastic card the cowling and radiator; glue them to the front of the fuselage and round off corners. From the same thickness card trace and cut out the tail-skid fairing and glue it to the rear of the fuselage. The raised machine-gun fairing is constructed from 0.25mm (0.010in.) plastic card and glued in front of the cockpit, and the edges faired in to the fuselage. Cut out a slot for the machine gun. Cut the head rest from plastic card as specified on the plan and score to help bending. Glue it to the fuselage where shown.

Shape the engine cylinder fairings from 3.0mm ($\frac{1}{8}$in.) birch dowel. Coat with polystyrene cement and smooth down. This will seal the grain in the wood for painting, and will enable them to be glued to the fuselage with solvent. Cut the exhaust pipes from plastic sprue and bend, holding them against a hot light bulb. Drill out the ends and glue them to the cylinder fairings with four short stubs cut from plastic rod glued in between each exhaust pipe.

Trace and cut out the wings, tail-plane, and rudder from 0.25mm (0.010in.) plastic card and construct them using the method described in the chapter on techniques. For this model the upper and lower wings are constructed in continuous lengths around 2.5mm ($\frac{3}{32}$in.) balsa sheet cores. The centre section in the upper wing is then cut using a razor saw and glued together over the plan to the correct angle.

Glue together both halves of the tail-plane assembly, making sure that the rib detail appears on the outside of each half. Score each side along the hinge line for the rudder and elevators to enable them to be set at any desired angle. Cut out the tail-skid from 1.00mm (0.040in.) plastic card and glue to the base of the rudder. Glue the tail-plane assembly to the fuselage and support with tape until set.

Trace and cut out from 0.50mm (0.020in.) plastic card the two under-carriage vee struts, together with the four centre section struts. Mark the strut positions on the fuselage. The undercarriage struts are glued into pre-cut slots, and the centre section struts bevelled and glued in place and held with Blu-Tack until set.

Cut out the axle from 0.50mm (0.020in.) plastic rod and the fairing from 0.25mm (0.010in.) plastic card. Score the rib detail on the inside halves. Score and fold over the axle and glue together. Align the axle in the undercarriage strut slots and glue.

Mark and cut out the ailerons in the wings and smooth edges.

Royal Aircraft Factory S.E.5a.

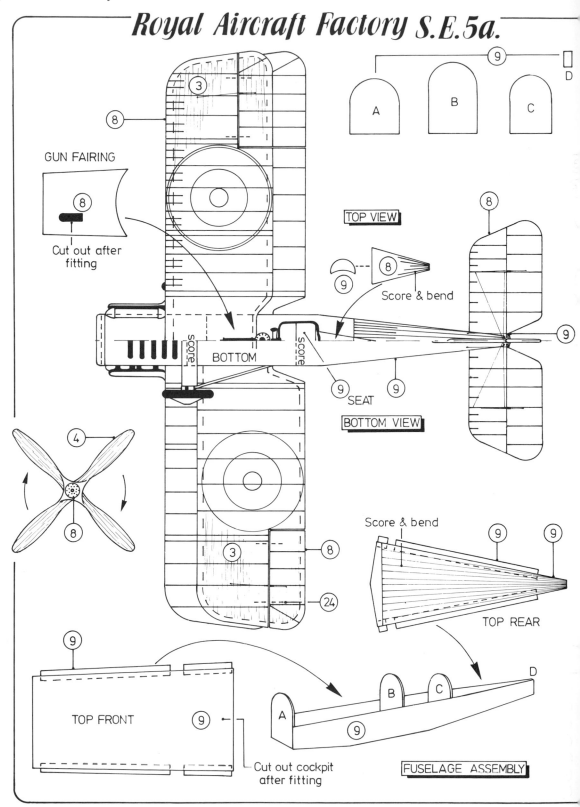

GUN FAIRING

Cut out after fitting

TOP VIEW

Score & bend

BOTTOM

score

score

SEAT

BOTTOM VIEW

A

B

C

D

Score & bend

TOP REAR

TOP FRONT

Cut out cockpit after fitting

A

B

C

D

FUSELAGE ASSEMBLY

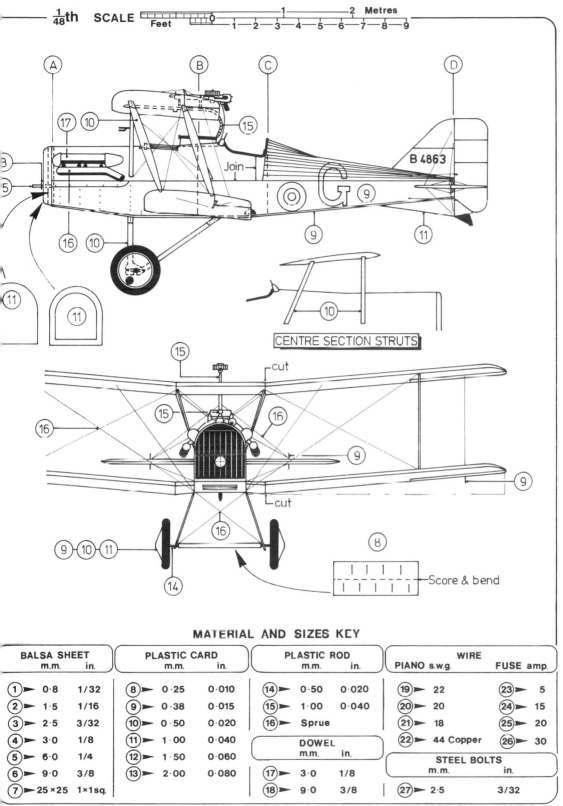

$\frac{1}{48}$th SCALE — Feet — Metres

A B C D

B 4863

Join

CENTRE SECTION STRUTS

cut

cut

Score & bend

MATERIAL AND SIZES KEY

BALSA SHEET m.m. in.	PLASTIC CARD m.m. in.	PLASTIC ROD m.m. in.	WIRE PIANO s.w.g. FUSE amp.
(1) 0·8 1/32	(8) 0·25 0·010	(14) 0·50 0·020	(19) 22 (23) 5
(2) 1·5 1/16	(9) 0·38 0·015	(15) 1·00 0·040	(20) 20 (24) 15
(3) 2·5 3/92	(10) 0·50 0·020	(16) Sprue	(21) 18 (25) 20
(4) 3·0 1/8	(11) 1·00 0·040	DOWEL m.m. in.	(22) 44 Copper (26) 30
(5) 6·0 1/4	(12) 1·50 0·060	(17) 3·0 1/8	STEEL BOLTS m.m. in.
(6) 9·0 3/8	(13) 2·00 0·080	(18) 9·0 3/8	(27) 2·5 3/32
(7) 25×25 1×1sq.			

Position the upper wing on top of the centre section struts and cut slots in the underside for the struts to be glued into. Mark the position of the lower wings and glue on the fuselage. Support the lower wings at the same angle with strips of tape attached to the upper wing. Measure and cut out the remaining outer wing struts from 0.50mm (0.020in.) plastic card and glue them into position. Remove tape when set.

Carve the propeller from two pieces of 3.00mm ($\frac{1}{8}$in.) sheet balsa joined together in the middle with a halving joint. Cut the propeller axle from 1.00mm (0.040in.) plastic rod and glue into a pre-drilled hole in the radiator.

The wheels are constructed from plastic card as specified. Spoke detail, which sometimes shows through the covering on the full size aircraft, is reproduced by filing flats on the moulded plastic card covers before gluing them to the wheels.

Cut out the control horns and pilot's seat from 0.38mm (0.015in.) plastic card and glue in place. The Foster gun-mounting is made from 1.00mm (0.040in.) plastic rod, bent by heating round a piece of suitable diameter dowel, filed to a square section, and glued on top of the centre wing section. Finally, form the cockpit padding from Blu-Tack coated with thinned polystyrene cement, or alternatively use modelling filler.

52 Centre section struts held with Blu-Tack while setting.

Finishing

The SE5a was flown by Major J.T.B. McCudden, Britain's fourth highest scoring pilot, with a reputed 57 victories, until his untimely death due to engine failure.

Colouring is khaki green overall except for the underside of the flying surfaces that are natural linen colour and includes the rear underside section of the fuselage up to just rear of the footstep.

Paint the inside of the cockpit light matt green, and the exhaust manifold, foster mounting, and machine-guns dark grey. The tyres are light grey with the valve accesses and radiator picked out in black. The wing, undercarriage, control horns, and cockpit padding are tan.

Stain the propeller with mahogany dye and apply two coats of sanding sealer and rub down. Finally finish with one or two coats of clear gloss varnish. Retain the propeller on the shaft with a boss cut from thin plastic card and paint dull silver.

Attach the ailerons with 15 amp. fuse-wire and set and glue to the required angle. Mark on the roundels with a pair of compasses and paint, including the vertical rudder stipes. Paint white the rear fuselage band. Use wet or dry transfer sheets for the serial number and the letter G. Mark on panel lines and stitching with a pencil and apply a coat of matt varnish overall. The oily metal exhaust pipes are represented by pencil smudges and coated with gloss varnish. Cut a suitable length of plastic rod for the gun site and glue the plastic sprue support bracket to the forward end; paint them both dark grey. Glue in position, together with the windscreen side supports made up from painted layers of P.V.A. glue. Glue on the wheels and machine guns. Fuse-wire is used for the pitot tube, and glued to the starboard wing strut and painted matt black. Apply the rigging and control wires, cut from stretched plastic sprue, starting at

53 Completed model ready for painting and detailing.

the centre section, then wings, tail-plane, and finally connect the control horns.

Cockpit details can be added if required. These include the instrument panel, made from plastic card, throttle levers and control column, made from fuse-wire. The pilot used on the model was bought, as were the machine guns, suitably painted and fitted.

54 Cockpit and Foster gun mounting detail.

sixteen
Felixstowe F2A Flying Boat

Introduction

The F2A was manufactured in this country by Saunders of Cowes, Isle of Wight, and other contractors under licence from the American designer Glen Curtiss. Major improvements were made to the British aircraft by Commander John Porte, who re-designed the hull arrangement and upswept tail-plane assembly, thus improving the planing performance for taking off and landing.

Twin 345 h.p. Rolls Royce Eagle engines replaced the less powerful Curtiss powerplants. Top speed, however, was still only 153 kmh (95 mph), with a slow rate of climb, contributed no doubt by the heavily constructed hull and large 29m (95ft) wingspan.

As the name implies, the aircraft was stationed at Felixstowe, and also Lowestoft and Great Yarmouth, although originally the aircraft was known as the Large America in the United States. Under the direction of Commander Porte, the Felixstowe entered service in December 1917 for reconnaissance and anti-submarine duties, including anti-Zeppelin patrols.

55 Felixstowe F2A.

Armament consisted of five Lewis gun positions. Three on top of the fuselage, including the open cockpit, and one in each side behind sliding fuselage hatches. Bombs were also carried and triggered from the forward gun position where the bomb aiming device was mounted.

Owing to its relatively large size in comparison with its smaller single-engined contemporaries, the model described here is built to $\frac{1}{72}$nd scale. The model can, however, also be constructed to $\frac{1}{48}$th scale by scaling up the plans using the method described at the beginning of this book. The material sizes must also be increased accordingly. Balsa wood is used for carving out the fuselage and floats. The flying surfaces, struts and engines are mainly constructed from plastic card and sprue.

Materials

Fuselage, 25 × 25mm (1 × 1in.) block balsa.
Fuselage floats, laminated 3.0mm ($\frac{1}{8}$in.) and 6.0mm ($\frac{1}{4}$in.) sheet balsa.
Wing floats, and engine blocks 6.0mm ($\frac{1}{4}$in.) sheet balsa.
Wing cores and propellers, 3.0mm ($\frac{1}{8}$in.) sheet balsa.
Flying surfaces, oil tanks and gun position lining, 0.25mm (0.010in.) plastic card.
Wing, tail-plane and engine struts, 0.50mm (0.020in.) plastic card.
Control horns, radiator surround, gravity wing tank top and engine mounting brackets, 0.50mm (0.020in.) plastic card.
Gravity wing tank bottom and radiators, 1.00mm (0.040in.) plastic card.
Wing stabilizer frame, 0.50mm (0.020in.) plastic rod.
Engine supports, exhausts and various fittings, plastic card, rod and sprue.
Windscreen, clear acetate sheet.
Control and rigging wires, 44 gauge copper wire.

Construction

Trace and cut out the fuselage profile from a suitable length of 25 × 25mm (1 × 1in.) block balsa, checking that all the sides are kept square. Trace the plan shape onto the block, and cut it out. Round off the corners using a template if necessary as a guide. Mark on the forward and aft gun positions, including the cockpit, and carve out from the top and underneath the fuselage.

Laminate two 6.0mm ($\frac{1}{4}$in.) and one 3.0mm ($\frac{1}{8}$in.) balsa sheets together for the fuselage float assembly. Trace and cut out the plan shape and curve the top lengthwise so that it fits under the fuselage. Mark the positions of the float steps from the plan and cut out and shape, starting at the bow and working aft. Mark the position of the fuselage on the floats and bevel the top of each side of the floats down towards the steps. Glue the floats to the underside of the fuselage and smooth down with fine glasspaper.

Cut out the upper and lower wing cores from 3.0mm ($\frac{1}{8}$in.)

sheet balsa and shape to an aerofoil section. Cover the surfaces with 0.25mm (0.010in.) plastic card with the rib detail scored on the insides. In view of the length of the upper wing I suggest that the plastic card is cut and joined at the centre. Do not try to fold the plastic card around the leading edges of the balsa cores as scoring the rib detail causes distortion on a wing of this length. Instead, cover the wing cores with two separate pieces and glue with solvent along the edges. Cut out the ailerons and seal edges with polystyrene cement.

Cut to length the lower wings and insert two 22g. piano-wire lugs into each wing root. Mark the position of each lower wing on the fuselage sides and push and glue the wings in place. Chock up the wings to the correct dihedral until the glue has set. Mark the positions of the struts between the float and underside of the lower wings. Cut and shape the struts from 0.50mm (0.020in.) plastic card, together with four 3.0mm ($\frac{1}{8}$in.) diameter float strut flanges, and glue in place.

Mark to length and cut out from 0.50mm (0.020in.) plastic card 14 interplane struts and glue them to the lower wings in the positions shown. Position the upper wing on top of the struts and support it with balsa blocks and an elastic band to hold in position while gluing the wing to the struts. The two centre section struts are shorter and are glued into the top of the fuselage.

Trace and cut out both halves of the tail-plane assembly from 0.25mm (0.010in.) plastic card and score the rib detail on the inside halves before gluing them together. Three layers of plastic card make up the required thickness of the fin and rudder. Cut a slot centrally in the tail-plane for the fin to fit in and glue.

56 Top wing held with balsa packing and elastic bands while setting.

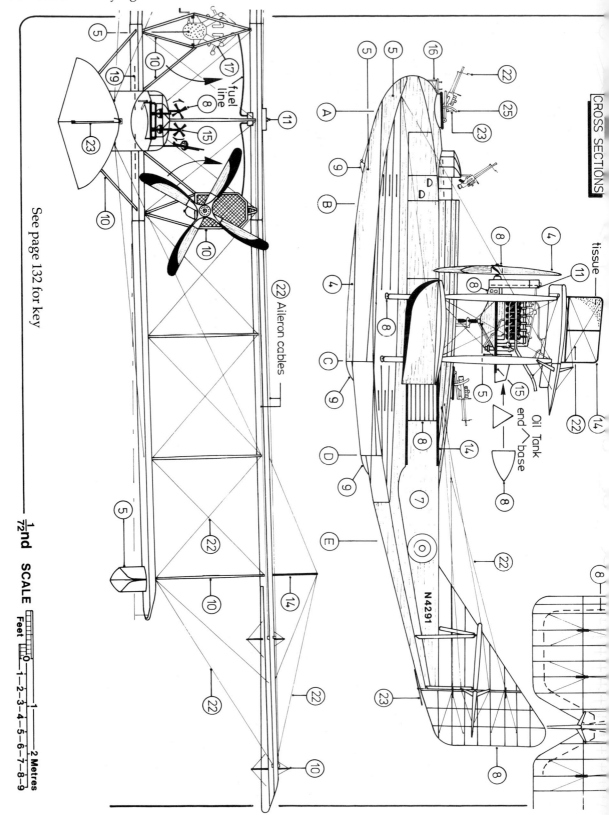

CROSS SECTIONS

See page 132 for key

$\frac{1}{72}$nd   SCALE

Feet
0 — 1 — 2 — 3 — 4 — 5 — 6 — 7 — 8 — 9
— 1 —   — 2 Metres

22 Aileron cables

fuel line

Oil Tank
end / base

tissue

N4291

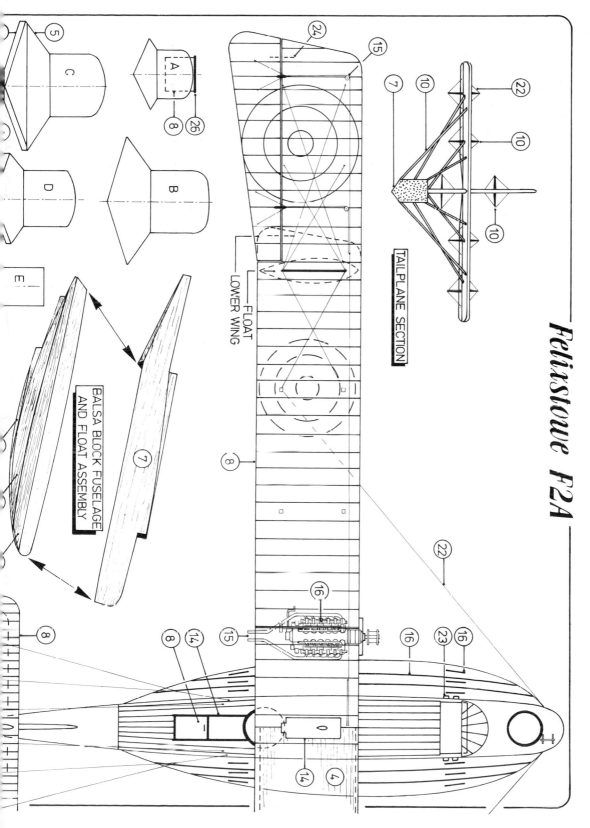

Felixstowe F2A

TAILPLANE SECTION

FLOAT
LOWER WING

BALSA BLOCK FUSELAGE
AND FLOAT ASSEMBLY

Glue the assembly to the rear of the fuselage and also four
struts, cut and shaped from 0.50mm (0.020in.) plastic card and
glued to each side between the underside of the tail-plane and
fuselage where shown.

Cut out and shape the two wing floats from 6.0mm ($\frac{1}{4}$in.)
sheet balsa. Seal the grain with two layers of polystyrene cement
and glue the wing floats to the lower wings in the position
shown.

Mount the two wing stabilizer frames, cut and bent from
0.50mm (0.020in.) plastic rod, into the upper wing and glue into
pre-drilled holes. The frames are covered with doped tissue
paper before painting.

Shape the two engine blocks and sumps from 6.0mm ($\frac{1}{4}$in.)
sheet balsa. Cut the 12 cylinders from 1.50mm (0.060in.) balsa
dowel for each engine and glue them to the blocks in a vee
formation. Form the exhaust pipes and other details from plastic
rod and sprue and glue into position. Each engine has a starting
handle mounted to the rear of the engine block and are each
handed facing towards the wing tips.

Trace and cut out the radiators from 1.00mm (0.040in.) plastic
card. Cut out the radiator surrounds from 0.50mm (0.020in.)
plastic card strips and glue around the radiator, leaving a
0.50mm rebate for gluing the grills into after painting. Cut the
radiator caps from 1.00mm (0.040in.) plastic rod and glue into

57 Engine strut detail.

position. Glue the radiators to the engine blocks by cutting off the propeller shaft housings and gluing them back onto the front of the radiators. Cut the engine mounting brackets from 0.50mm (0.020in.) plastic card and glue them to each side of the engine blocks. Glue the radiator mounting brackets, cut from 0.25mm (0.010in.) plastic card, between the rear bottom corners of each radiator and the forward ends of the engine mounting brackets. Note the lightening holes, which should be drilled before the brackets are glued in place.

Cut to length and shape the engine struts from plastic card as specified. Glue in position first the two vee struts for each engine to the lower wing, checking that they are the same width at the top as the engine mounting brackets. Connect the vee struts together with the engine supports cut from 1.00mm (0.040in.) plastic rod and filed flat. Temporarily hold the engines in position with Blu-Tack while the remaining struts are glued in place except the inverted vee struts, which are glued directly to the front of the cylinders. The top of the struts are not glued to the upper wing at this stage so you can remove the engines for painting. Cut out the oil tanks from plastic card as specified and assemble them. Glue the tanks behind each engine on top of the supports.

Construct the two four-bladed propellers from 3.0mm ($\frac{1}{8}$in.) sheet balsa. First cut to size four lengths of balsa the same diameter as the propellers and glue them together centrally with a halving joint to form a cross. Mark out and shape each blade, noting the handed rotation of each propeller and pitch. Cut the propeller shafts from suitable plastic rod and glue them into pre-drilled holes in the ends of the engine shaft housings.

Trace and cut out the control horns (20 will be required) and the upper and lower parts of the gravity tank from plastic card as specified and glue them in the positions shown. The airscrew driven petrol pumps are made from scrap plastic card and sprue and glued in place after the painting is finished.

58 Engine construction.

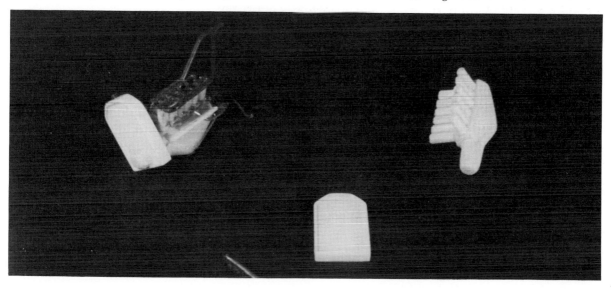

Finishing

Standard finish on most aricraft consisted of dark green fuselage and upper flying surfaces with natural linen colour under sides. The fuselage washboards and nose, being timber covered, were varnished. A few aircraft were dazzle painted in chevron and horizontal stripe formations, supposedly to frighten the opposition. Colours varied and sometimes incorporated the roundel colours, and also yellow, green or black.

The model represented here is serial No. N4291 and is finished in standard colours. Owing to the considerable amount of detail the painting and finishing sequence is listed numerically as follows:

1. Stain with mahogany dye, fuselage sides, nose, and propeller hubs.
2. Apply two coats of sanding sealer to fuselage and propellers, and smooth down.
3. Apply two coats of gloss varnish to above.
4. Cut from 0.25mm (0.010in.) plastic card the two gun position linings and float fin, and glue in position.
5. Cut from 30 amp. fuse-wire gun well rims, and bend and glue them on to top of linings.
6. Cut from plastic rod float battens and footruns, and glue on.
7. Dope on light weight tissue-covering to upper wing tip stabilizer frames and trim.
8. Paint underside of flying surfaces cream.
9. Mark out positions of washboards, nose, and front decking, which remains varnished, and paint dark green the remainder of the fuselage, fin, and upper flying surfaces.
10. Paint dark brown all struts and control horns. The inside and outside of the gun linings are tan coloured with light grey rims.
11. Paint grey float battens and footruns, wing tank, oil tanks, and float strut flanges.
12. Mark out and paint roundels, rudder stripes, and apply the serial number using dry transfers.
13. Mark on fuselage panelling the rib detail and cockpit footstep recesses with a ruling pen.
14. Coat entire model with semi-gloss clear varnish.
15. Cut out three gun port-doors from 0.25mm (0.010in.) plastic card and runners from plastic rod; paint and glue them in position.
16. Paint grey propeller blades with brass coloured tips and leading edges.
17. Measure and cut out paper templates of the windscreen top and bottom sections. Trace and cut out from clear acetate sheet, score, bend, and glue in position. Paint frames green.
18. Paint engines: crankcases — dull silver; cylinders and exhaust piping — dark grey; and radiators — matt black with grey surrounds. Score radiator grills with a knife.
19. Construct fuel lines from polyester yarn and paint grey.
20. Glue engines in position and connect fuel lines to lower half of the wing tank.

21 Paint grey the two airscrew-driven petrol pumps and glue side by side on top of the fuselage between the two centre section struts.

22 Construct the two machine-gun scarff rings from 20 amp. fuse-wire, bent around balsa dowel to shape. Notch and bend the elevation supports also from 20 amp. fuse-wire and glue assemblies to the well rims. Represent the bungy cord with 5 amp. fuse-wire. Paint scarff ring assemblies grey and the bungy cords matt black.

23 Suitably paint the pilot and co-pilot plus two crew figures and fit complete with twin wheel type control columns made from 5 amp. fuse-wire, painted grey.

24 Paint the machine-guns dark grey and glue them to scarff rings and through the port side of windscreen. Twin guns are featured in the nose on the model.

25 Construct the bomb-aiming and trigger mechanism from plastic rod and sprue; paint grey and glue them on the starboard side of the nose.

26 Cut the four cockpit steps from 5 amp. fuse-wire; bend to shape and glue into the sides of the fuselage and paint grey.

27 Glue bow and stern strops, cut from 5 amp. fuse-wire, to underside of hull and paint them grey.

28 Construct a display stand as described in the chapter on displaying models. This should be done at this stage as it supports the model while the rigging is being applied.

29 Add cockpit details that will be visible. The prototype model featured a map and compass mounted on the console.

30 Measure and cut pre-rolled 44 swg copper wire for the rigging. Glue in position, starting at the centre section, working out towards the wing tips. Next, apply the upper wing tip and control horn bracing and then the external control wires

59 Cockpit and forward gun position.

between the tail-plane and fuselage. Lastly, glue the external aileron control wires along both sides of the leading edge of the upper wing, complete with pulleys made from plastic rod, and glue the drag wires between the wings and fuselage.

31 Construct the pitot tube from 5 amp. fuse-wire and glue it to the forward strut second in from the port wing tip.

32 Slip on the two propellers, noting the direction of rotation and blade pitch. Retain them with a boss on each shaft made from thin plastic card, painted grey.

MATERIAL AND SIZES KEY

BALSA SHEET			PLASTIC CARD			PLASTIC ROD			WIRE			
m.m.	in.		m.m.	in.		m.m.	in.		PIANO s.w.g.		FUSE amp.	
(1)► 0·8	1/32		(8)► 0·25	0·010		(14)► 0·50	0·020		(19)► 22		(23)►	5
(2)► 1·5	1/16		(9)► 0·38	0·015		(15)► 1·00	0·040		(20)► 20		(24)►	15
(3)► 2·5	3/32		(10)► 0·50	0·020		(16)► Sprue			(21)► 18		(25)►	20
(4)► 3·0	1/8		(11)► 1·00	0·040		DOWEL			(22)► 44 Copper		(26)►	30
(5)► 6·0	1/4		(12)► 1·50	0·060		m.m.	in.		STEEL BOLTS			
(6)► 9·0	3/8		(13)► 2·00	0·080		(17)► 3·0	1/8		m.m.		in.	
(7)►25×25	1×1sq.					(18)► 9·0	3/8		(27)► 2·5		3/32	

III Displaying and Photographing Models

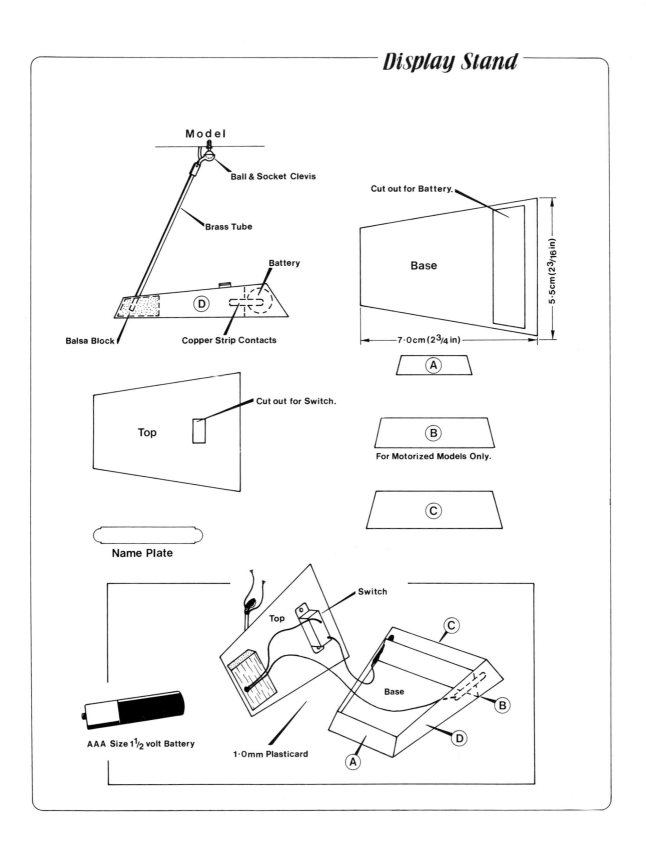

Model

Ball & Socket Clevis

Brass Tube

Battery

Balsa Block

Copper Strip Contacts

D

Cut out for Battery.

Base

5·5cm (2³/₁₆in)

7·0cm (2³/₄ in)

A

Top

Cut out for Switch.

B

For Motorized Models Only.

C

Name Plate

Switch

Top

C

Base

B

D

A

AAA Size 1½ volt Battery

1·0mm Plasticard

seventeen

How to Photograph your Models

With their exposed rigging and bracing, models of the First World War tend to be susceptible to damage if mishandled. They can also be just as easily damaged when removing dust or by cleaning. It is advisable, therefore, to display them in a way which not only sets the model off to advantage but also protects them against accidental damage and general deterioration.

This chapter suggests various ways of displaying the models and some ideas on making a diorama. Photography provides a permanent record of these models and indeed can be a most rewarding branch of the hobby, not only from a personal point of view but also as a potential source of income from model magazines where good quality photographs of projects are invited for publication. Techniques are explained for setting up different shots and the equipment required.

Stand

Page 135 shows a display stand suitable for most $\frac{1}{48}$th scale models. Plastic card is used to build the base, sides, and top, with a brass tube support. A ball and socket clevis, of the type used for linkages in radio-controlled models, enables the model to be displayed at various angles. The ball end of the clevis is glued into a pre-drilled hole in the underside of the fuselage at the centre of balance, with the socket end glued and bent to the required angle into the top of the brass tube support.

A small piece of Blu-Tack stuck into the base of the socket provides the necessary tension. The stand can be painted any colour; black enamel, however, followed by a coat of clear matt varnish will complement the colour schemes of most models. A name plate will give that finishing touch. This can be made from thin plastic card and suitably painted; brass or copper enamel is quite effective. Dry transfer sheets, obtainable in various styles of lettering, are used for applying the letters followed by a coat of clear gloss varnish. The completed name plate is then glued to the angled front of the stand.

Where models are motorized the same stand in a modified form as shown is suitable for housing a small 1.5V. battery and on/off switch. Fine, twin-flex connecting wire is threaded through small holes made in the socket from the model, down inside the tube support, into the base and wired to a small switch screwed into the top of the base. The battery contacts are made from copper or brass strip and glued to the inside. Access to the battery is through a rectangular hole cut in the base of the stand. (*See also* Albatros D111 project page 89.)

Showcases

These can be bought in various shapes and sizes in either perspex or glass with wood or aluminium frames. The thin metal-framed glass cases offer maximum visibility and can be supplied with different coloured bases and optional mirrors to substitute one or more of the glass panels. If the model is to be displayed on a stand, this must be taken into account when determining the height of the case. A suitable case can be made at home with L shaped wooden mouldings for the frames, and clear perspex panels; cut them to size with a tenon saw. Plywood is used for the base, which can be painted or covered with material.

Blow brush

Even under cover the models may need dusting occasionally. As well as gentle blowing, a blow brush of the type used to remove dust on camera lenses is ideal.

Dioramas

A suitable background can make a model look realistic and create a certain atmosphere. This is certainly true with early aircraft when placed in an airfield setting. The simplest form of setting is a photograph from a magazine or a poster placed inside the back of the showcase. Another method which is very effective is to build a 3D setting with tents and trees etc. These items can be obtained commercially as model train and army accessories or built from scratch.

60 Models displayed in a commercially made showcase.

To begin with a base board and vertical back is required. This can be either cardboard or plywood, depending on whether you require a permanent display or just a temporary arrangement for photographing. Stick blue or grey paper (obtainable from art supplies) to the backing board for the sky, creating cloud effects with aerosol spray paint. Cover the base with a sand and saw-dust mixture. Figures, suitably painted and posed, can also be incorporated and the whole scene housed in a showcase for protection.

Photography

Camera
The ideal camera for this type of photography is the 35mm single reflex type which enables the subject to be viewed and focused directly through the viewfinder.

Lenses, hood, cable release, tripod
Lenses of around 28 and 80mm focal lengths are suitable. A single macro zoom lens, however, which combines these two lengths, is preferable as this will give a range of shots from a moderate wide angle to a moderate telephoto for close up work without your having to move the camera backwards and forwards.

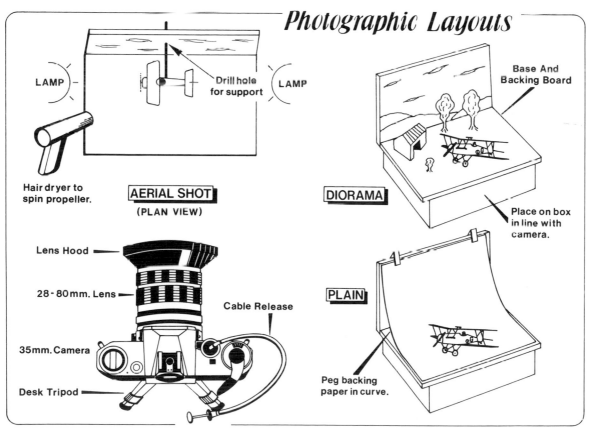

Photographic Layouts

LAMP
Drill hole for support
LAMP
Hair dryer to spin propeller.
AERIAL SHOT
(PLAN VIEW)

Lens Hood
28-80mm. Lens
Cable Release
35mm. Camera
Desk Tripod

Base And Backing Board
DIORAMA
Place on box in line with camera.

PLAIN
Peg backing paper in curve.

The models can be photographed outside on a table but choose an overcast day rather than bright sunlight because of problems with shadows. Taking indoor shots under artificial light requires a small desk top tripod together with a cable release to avoid camera shake at low shutter speeds. A rubber lens hood is useful for reducing glare from the side when using lamps and also gives some protection to the lens itself if accidentally knocked.

Lighting

Lighting need not be any more elaborate than two or three table lamps fitted with 100 or 150 watt bulbs. These are positioned on each side of the model to eliminate shadows and adjusted whilst you look through the viewfinder.

Coloured paper

Coloured paper can be used for photographing models against plain backgrounds. The colour should complement the model — for example, the red Fokker Triplane is photographed against green paper, and the dark green camouflage of the SE5a contrasts well against a yellow background. To avoid an unsightly join line the paper is draped from the back down in a gentle curve below where the model is placed. A cardboard box with a flap-type top is suitable for supporting the paper. The box also serves as a platform to enable the camera lens to be positioned at the same level as the model to give a more dramatic 'worm's eye' view.

Diorama

Diorama are photographed in the same way on a box to bring the lens to the same level as the model and lit from the sides if you are photographing indoors. Trees and other items of scenery can easily form shadows on the backdrop, so positioning of the lamps is quite critical. Unwanted reflections can be a problem; these originate from polished engine cowlings or the wire rigging, but moving the model very slightly will usually solve this. Also watch out for reflections from backdrops if they are posters of blow-ups of photographs that have shiny surfaces.

Aerial shots

Aerial shots can be taken against photograph blow-ups of clouds or scenes. Posters are a good source of material, or pictures taken through aircraft windows when you're going on holiday. The background picture must be attached to a sturdy board to enable a metal rod support to be held in position through a pre-drilled hole. The other end is attached to the model with tape in a suitable flying attitude. The trick here is to align the camera so that the support is invisible in the viewfinder; the model may have to be adjusted several times before everything looks all right. Care must also be taken to see that the support does not throw a shadow onto the background when lit. Just before the shutter is released spin the propeller, either by flicking it with a finger or using a hair dryer.

Depth of field

This is the nearest and furthest points of the subject which are in focus. If, for example, you want the entire model to be in focus, select a small aperture of around f16. When using this setting in artificial light, with the wattage lamps previously mentioned, the shutter speed will be quite slow at around one quarter of a second at 100 ASA film speed rating.

For highlighting a certain part of a model or blurring the foreground or background in a scene, given the same lighting level, an aperture of around f5–6 or wider should be selected with a shutter speed of around $\frac{1}{30}$th of a second. You will need to use a tripod and cable release with these slow shutter speeds. If photographing outdoors the shutter speeds will be considerably higher and the camera can be hand held down to speeds of $\frac{1}{25}$th of a second.

The above settings are only an example of the many combinations that can be used, and therefore I suggest that you take several shots of one scene with different settings and note the results. Many cameras nowadays can be used in the automatic or manual mode so do try both, as experimenting is half the fun in photographing models.

Aircraft Anatomy

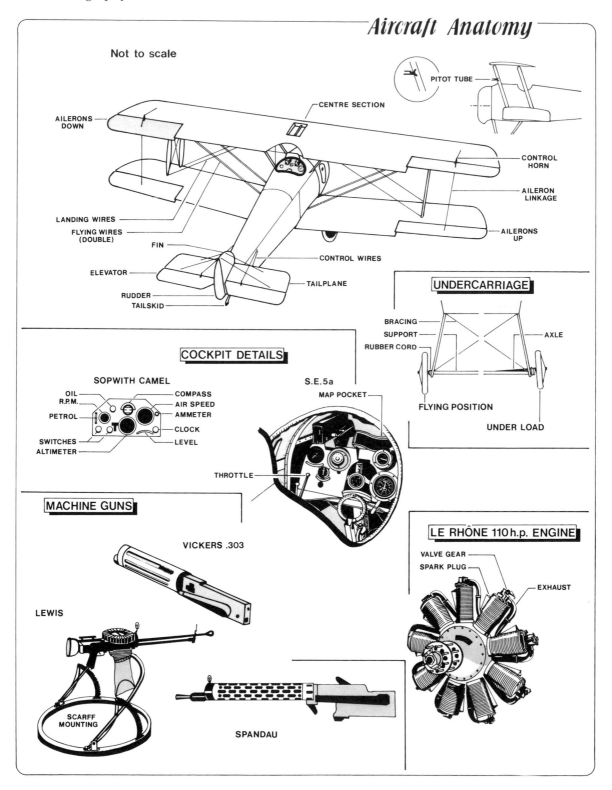

Not to scale

PITOT TUBE

AILERONS DOWN

CENTRE SECTION

CONTROL HORN

AILERON LINKAGE

LANDING WIRES

FLYING WIRES (DOUBLE)

FIN

AILERONS UP

CONTROL WIRES

ELEVATOR

TAILPLANE

RUDDER

TAILSKID

UNDERCARRIAGE

BRACING

SUPPORT

RUBBER CORD

AXLE

FLYING POSITION

UNDER LOAD

COCKPIT DETAILS

SOPWITH CAMEL

OIL
R.P.M.

PETROL

SWITCHES

ALTIMETER

COMPASS

AIR SPEED

AMMETER

CLOCK

LEVEL

S.E.5a

MAP POCKET

THROTTLE

MACHINE GUNS

VICKERS .303

LEWIS

SCARFF MOUNTING

SPANDAU

LE RHÔNE 110 h.p. ENGINE

VALVE GEAR

SPARK PLUG

EXHAUST

Bibliography

Cambell, Christopher, *Aces And Aircraft of World War 1*
Treasure Press, 1984

Cheeseman, E.F., *Fighter Aircraft of the 1914–18 War*
Harleyford Publications Ltd, Letchworth, Herts. 1960

Chesneau, Roger, *Scale Models in Plastic*
Conway Maritime Press Ltd. 1979

Ellis, Chris, *The Scale Modellers Handbook* The Hamlyn
Publishing Group Ltd. 1979

Hedges, Martin, *Model Aircraft*
The Hamlyn Publishing Group Ltd. 1979

Gray, Peter, L. and Stair, Ian, R., *Fokker Fighters of World War 1*
Wingspan Publications, Vintage Aviation Publications Ltd.
Oxford. 1976

Gray, Peter, L. and Stair, Ian, R., *Albatros Fighters of World War 1*
Wingspan Publications, Vintage Aviation Publications Ltd,
Oxford, 1979

Smeed, Vic, *The Encyclopedia of Model Aircraft*
Octopus Books Ltd. 1979

Tanner, John, *British Military Aircraft of World War One*
Arms and Armour Press, 1976

Suppliers

All materials specified for these models are generally available from most good model shops. In case of difficulty and for specialized items, some addresses are given below.

United Kingdom

Bev's Models, 35 West Street, Bedminster, Bristol. (0272) 662544

Model Mania, 17 King Street, Cambridge. (0223) 359620

Exeter Model Centre Ltd, 39 Sidwell Street, Exeter, Devon. (0392) 35118

E.M. Models, 42–4 Camden Road, Tunbridge Wells, Kent. (0892) 36689

Stan Catchpole's Model World, 85 Bold Street, Liverpool. (051) 709 8093

Modelcraft, 2 Paigle Road, Aylestone, Leicester. (0533) 836649

Henry J. Nicholls and Son Ltd, 308 Holloway Road, London N7 (01) 607 4272

Red Baron Models Ltd, 497 Hertford Road, Enfield, Middx. (01) 804 7452

Dunns Models, 3 West Nile Street, Glasgow, Scotland. (041) 221 0484

Swansea Models and Hobbies, Plymouth Street, Swansea, Wales. (0792) 52877

Bob's Models, 520–2 Coventry Road, Small Heath, Birmingham 10 (021) 772 4917

Three Towers Models, 58 Haley Hill, Boothdown Road, Halifax, Yorks. (0422) 44403

Balsa wood
Solarbro Balsa, Commerce Way, Lancing, Sussex. (0903) 752866

Plastic sheet
EMA Model Supplies Ltd, 58–60 The Centre, Feltham, Middx. (01) 890 5270

Paint, transfers, white metal fittings and figures
Hannants, 56 London Road North, Lowestoft, Suffolk. (0502) 65688

Creative Crafts, 11 The Square, Winchester SO23 9ES

Showcases
Gulliver Showcases, Unit 7, 82–6 Cambridge Road, Stansted, Essex. (0279) 816316

U.S.A.

Hobby Barn, P.O. Box 17856, Tucson, Arizona 85731.

Archer's Hobby World, P.O. Box 297, Atwood, California 92601.

Sheldon's Hobby Shop, 3157 Alum Rock Avenue, San Jose, California 95127.

Al's R/C Supplies, 54 Chesnut Hill Road, Norwalk, Connecticut.

Carl Wilson's Clear Track Ltd. 3506 Palm Beach Road, Fort Myers, Florida.

Hobby Junction, 3260 South Cobb Drive, Smyrna, Georgia.

Tower Hobbies, P.O. Box 778, Champain, Illinois 61820.

Penn Valley Hobby Centre, 837 W. Main Street, Lansdale, Pennsylvania 19446

J And J's Hobbies, Inc, 785 Broadway, Kingston, New York.

High Sierra Models, 953 W. Moana Lane, Reno, Nevada.

Central Hobby Supply, 915 Olive, Room 214, St Louis, Montana 63101.

Larry's Hobbies, 2114 E. FM 1960, Houston, Texas.

Balsa wood
Balsa U.S.A., P.O. Box 164, Marinette, Wisconsin 54143.

Plastic sheet
1st Armored Model Supply Company, P.O. Box 1706, New Rochelle, New York 10802.

Miniature tools
Micro-Mark, P.O. Box 5112PB, 24 East Main Street, Clinton, New Jersey 08809.

Index